My friend, classmate and colleague, the Reverend Dr. Stephen Lomax has written an excellent book, entitled *Just Wait 'Til Your Daddy Gets Home*. If you are concerned about the plight of fatherless homes and the impact they have on society; I recommend that you read this book.

Dr. Lomax has done an outstanding job in giving an analysis of what mothers, fathers, children and all of us involved in molding and shaping the lives of our young men should do to sustain the family. Please get a copy of this insightful book and be blessed!

—Reverend Dr. James Blassingame, Pastor of the Mount Zion Missionary Baptist Church, Sumter, S. C Vice-President at Large, Baptist E&M Convention of S.C. First Assistant Secretary, National Baptist Convention, USA, Inc.

In his Book entitled *Just Wait "Til Your Daddy gets home*

Dr. Lomax highlights the statistics of young men growing up without a positive role model in the home and the resulting negative effects.

Also, he addresses the need for women to make better decisions when it comes to choosing life partners, because of the consequences that none committed men have on their children.

He further states that in the final analysis of it all, it is the children, especially the young men who are affected most by the presence or absence of a Father and give practical solutions as well as biblical truth for reversing the down spiral of our families. Every father and every person concerned about the role of fathers and the family must read this book.

—Reverend Robert Lee Mcgowens, Senior pastor of the Greater Galilee Baptist Church, Charlotte, N. C.

I want to thank Dr. Stephen Lomax for addressing a plight in our society that is affecting the downward spiral of our country and world. Until humanity again puts all it has back into the hands of the Creator and realize that humans are stewards of all God has given, including the children He blessed mankind with; that they too are from God and man must give an account of the stewardship in parenting them.

In his latest book, entitled, *Just Wait 'Til Your Daddy Gets Home,* Dr. Lomax has been very Biblically factual and socially straight forward in dealing with the real life issues of the family. Thank you for putting this country on notice from the pulpit. All people concerned with the plight of the family must attain a copy of this book.

—Reverend James Clark, M. Div.;
First Vice Moderator Union #1 RRBA, Honorary
UNCF Chairperson Upstate, Pastor, Wilson
Calvary Baptist Church, Anderson, S.C.

Dr. Stephen Lomax has written another book to enhance and enlighten reader's concerning the plight of the family. In the book, he is very transparent concerning his own journey and the obstacles he faced in his own life. He raises some unique questions and observations about the family that grabs the attention of the reader.

Just Wait 'Til Your Daddy Gets Home is a unique book filled with insight and data analysis that informs the reader concerning the dilemmas of the family. It is a great book for the entire family to read.

—Dr. Reginald Dawkins
Pastor/Founder of Triumph Christian Center
Newport News, Hampton Va. Adjunct Professor at
Hampton University, Hampton, Va.

Finally a book that lies out concrete evidence and unmistakably defines the negative consequences of homes without fathers. This book touches on the statistics of rape, imprisonment, murders, school dropouts, teen pregnancy and other problems; to help you grasp the severity of absentee fathers.

Doctor Lomax has created his greatest work to date in this book. With only the first words read my mind took me back to the days of my childhood where I too marched to the drum beat of those words, "Just wait 'til your daddy gets home." Momma used to say them to me and my brothers and sisters and immediately we became agreeable and attentive.

Anyone reading this book will come away with a real sense of what is wrong with America and the World; the absence of the father figures in the home is a major contributor. All fathers, mothers and children must read this book.

Doctor Lomax; thanks for calling a spade a spade and not wavering on such a crucial issue and "telling it like it is." Particularly revealing some of your own personal experiences which further compelled you address such a terrible problem in society today.

—Reverend Harold W. Chapman
Pastor, Pine Grove AMEC
Greenwood, S.C.

A must read! Dr. Lomax has captured the true meaning of fatherhood. The title of the book takes us back to the culture of discipline and accountability in the home.

Dr. Lomax has demonstrated that as the father goes, so goes society. The book offers every reader a critical and affirming analysis of the hero of the home.

—Reverend James Hailstock, pastor of the
New Day Baptist Church, Spartanburg, S. C.

"Just wait 'til your daddy gets home!" is a phrase so powerful and so well known that both the young and old know what it means! The title compels you to look inside and the contents will implore you to explore this writing from cover to cover. Dr. Stephen Lomax addresses an issue that affects everyone, regardless of race, creed, religion or even their social-economic status.

In the book *Just Wait 'Til Your Daddy Gets Home*, Dr. Lomax goes far beyond the cold facts of statistics to call our attention to the problems of fatherless homes. He draws on his experience as a member of both the Greenville County Detention Center Review Board and the South Carolina Juvenile Probation and Parole Board.

For many writers that would be enough, but Dr. Lomax is a man of God and as such he takes us to God's Word concerning man and his role of importance and authority in the family! And just to show how much this subject means to him, he shares the impact that his absent father had on him, each of his siblings and mother. I strongly believe, once you read this book, you will be pricked to your soul whenever you hear the words, "Just wait "til your daddy gets home!"

—Jerry B. Alexander Sr.
Pastor – Union Missionary Baptist Church
St. Petersburg, Fl.

Dr. Lomax has done a masterful job of detailing the diagnosis of what continues to be a spreading epidemic particularly in American society—fatherless homes. Having the courage to share the personal experiences of his childhood in what became the single-parent home of nine children is particularly impactful.

While we've all heard the devastating statistics of children reared in single-parent households, his treatment of this information along with his own testimony leaves every reader—especially fathers—convicted and moved to act. I pray that this book serves as a wake-up call to every man, father, and husband. It's time for daddies to come back home!

—Reverend Curtis Johnson, pastor of the
Valley Brook Baptist Church, Ware Place, S. C.

Dr. Lomax is an example of a preacher/pastor who combines an anointed spirit, an educated mind, and a passion for preaching and teaching God's word. I recommend this book because it is well researched and blended together with riveting personal insight.

There is no way anyone can read this book without being touched in a profound manner. Congratulations to Dr. Lomax for not only a well-written book, but congratulations for overcoming the odds and the challenges in his life to find great success.

We give God the praise for all that He has done, but it takes one who will place Himself in the will of God as Dr. Lomax has for God to lift them out the difficult circumstances of life. My prayer is that men whether fathers or not will read this book as it shows the consequences of our actions, but also shows that there is always hope in God. You must get a copy of this New Book!

—Dr. Phillip Baldwin, Pastor of the Bethlehem
Baptist Church, Simpsonville, S. C. Moderator
of the Reedy River Baptist Association

Just Wait
'Til Your Daddy Gets Home

Just Wait
'Til Your Daddy Gets Home

Stephen Samuel Lomax

TATE PUBLISHING
AND ENTERPRISES, LLC

Just Wait 'Til Your Daddy Gets Home
Copyright © 2012 by Stephen Samuel Lomax. All rights reserved.

No part of this publication may be reproduced, stored in a retrieval system or transmitted in any way by any means, electronic, mechanical, photocopy, recording or otherwise without the prior permission of the author except as provided by USA copyright law.

This book is designed to provide accurate and authoritative information with regard to the subject matter covered. This information is given with the understanding that neither the author nor Tate Publishing, LLC is engaged in rendering legal, professional advice. Since the details of your situation are fact dependent, you should additionally seek the services of a competent professional.

The opinions expressed by the author are not necessarily those of Tate Publishing, LLC.

Published by Tate Publishing & Enterprises, LLC
127 E. Trade Center Terrace | Mustang, Oklahoma 73064 USA
1.888.361.9473 | www.tatepublishing.com

Tate Publishing is committed to excellence in the publishing industry. The company reflects the philosophy established by the founders, based on Psalm 68:11,
"The Lord gave the word and great was the company of those who published it."

Book design copyright © 2012 by Tate Publishing, LLC. All rights reserved.
Cover design by Lauro Talibong
Interior design by Mary Jean Archival

Published in the United States of America

ISBN: 978-1-62295-316-5
1. Biography & Autobiography, General
2. Family & Relationships, Family Relationships
12.10.23

Contents

Foreword 13
Acknowledgements 15
The Purpose of Book 19

Chapter I 21
    Introduction

Chapter II 27
    The Impact of Fatherlessness On The Fatherless!

Chapter III 53
    Biblically Speaking!
    Get Back To The Basics of The Bible! Father's Basic Roles!
    Provider

Chapter IV 63
    What Might Have Been!
    (Had Daddy Been There, Only God Knows?)

Chapter V 91
    Daddy's Home!
    The Importance Of The Father's Presence!
    (In The Children's Own Words)

Chapter VI 121
    How To Attain And Maintain Loving Families!
    Cohabitation Is Not One Of Them
    Beyonce' Has A Point!
    The Importance Of Two Parent System!
    (Husband And Wife, Male And Female)
    Everybody's Has A Part To Play!

Chapter VII 133
   How To Attain And Maintain Loving Families, Part Two!
   What's Children Got To With It?
   Everybody's Has A Part To Play, Including The Children

Chapter VIII 147
   Father Of The Fatherless! What To Do
   When Daddy Doesn't Come Home!
   Make the Best out of a Bad situation!

Chapter IX 157
   Children Caught In The Middle
   Stop The Fighting (For The Children's Sake!)

Chapter X 169
   What You Don't Know Can Hurt You!

Foreword

Dr. Stephen Lomax has hit a home run with this book and has put his finger on the great need in America. Our families are crumbling and falling apart and we need help. Dr. Lomax has given us a true picture of today's family and then the solution to get it turned around.

Dr. Lomax is a man of character and integrity and loves the family. I believe this book will impact your life, your family and America, if prayerfully and carefully read and its truths applied.

—Reverend Dr. David Gallamore, Pastor of the
Rock Springs Baptist Church, Easley, S. C.

"Just wait 'til your daddy gets home!" is a phrase so powerful and so well known that both the young and old know what it means! The title compels you to look inside and the contents will implore you to explore this writing from cover to cover. Dr. Stephen Lomax addresses an issue that affects everyone, regardless of race, creed, religion or even their social-economic status.

In the book *Just Wait 'Til Your Daddy Gets Home*, Dr. Lomax goes far beyond the cold facts of statistics to call our attention to the problems of fatherless homes. He draws on his experience as a member of both the Greenville County Detention Center Review Board and the South Carolina Juvenile Probation and Parole Board.

For many writers that would be enough, but Dr. Lomax is a man of God and as such he takes us to God's Word concerning man and his role of importance and authority in the family! And just to show how much this subject means to him, he shares the impact that his absent father had on him, each of his siblings and mother. I strongly believe, once you read this book, you will be pricked to your soul whenever you hear the words, "Just wait "til your daddy gets home!"

—Jerry B. Alexander Sr.
Pastor – Union Missionary Baptist Church
St. Petersburg, Fl.

Acknowledgements

First, I must acknowledge God, the Father, God the Son and God, the Holy Spirit for the inspiration and motivation, energy, courage, confidence and knowledge to write the book. If it had not been for the Lord in my life, I don't know what I would do!

Second, I thank God for the love, support and longevity of Mrs. Frances Delores Shaw Lomax. Your love and spiritual leadership has been superior down through the thirty-nine years of marriage.

May God richly bless you; if it had not been for you, I don't know what I would do? Thanks so much for all you do. From the depths of my heart and soul, I love you. Riding the rollercoaster of life with you has been great.

To my children, Africa, Kenya, Stephanie and Jerrell, I love you with agape (God's unlimited and non-expectant) love. Over the years, you have brought your mother and me so much pride and joy that all of the money at Fort Knox could not buy. Love Ya!

To my two sons in law (Todd and Jaron), you have added much to the Lomax family and I am proud to call you not only sons in law, but sons. Keep up the good work and may God bless you and your family as well.

To my grandchildren, Stephen Samuel Lomax, II (Nuke), Zhain Mckensie Roux (Ms. Roux), and Zion Madison, if I had only known what emotions of joy and fulfillment you would bring to my heart, I would have had you first.

I cannot put into words, the deep love and happiness I feel just looking at you. Stay close so that I can see you regularly and participate in your lives. Additionally, I have been blessed with a fourth beautiful grand daughter, Frances Amani McComb. The Blessings just keep on coming.

To all of my dearly beloved brothers, Robert and his daughter Ola Louise; James Willie, (Dot), Joe Louis and my only remaining sister, Judy and her husband, James (Boot) Irby; thanks so much for the defense, love and support over the years. It meant and still means so much to me. Also, thanks to your children, my nephew James and nieces, Jackie, Julie and Jatavia for their support.

To all of the members of the New Life in Christ Missionary Baptist Church, mere words cannot describe the love, respect and admiration I have for you. I am one of the few that have been blessed with both of God's two institutions; a great biological family and a great church family. Thank you so much for your commitment to righteousness in 2005 and continuance stance today.

You exemplify the words of the prophet Amos. He said, "Let justice run down as waters and righteousness as a mighty stream" (Amos 5: 24 KJvSV). I will never forget your dedication, devotion and support. "A family that prays together stays together." May heaven continue to smile upon you, your families and the New Life in Christ Baptist Church; I know I will.

I must thank Reverend Minister Isaiah D. Thomas, Stellar Award Winner,; Dr. David Galloway, pastor of the Rock Springs Baptist church, Easley S. C. for the foreword; Reverend Dr. James Blassingame, First vice president of the S. C. E. & M Convention; Reverend Dr. Phillip Baldwin, pastor of the Bethlehem Baptist church, Simpsonville, S. C; Reverend Robert Mcgowens, senior pastor of the Greater Galilee Baptist Church, Charlotte, N. C.

Thanks also to the Reverend Jerry Alexander, pastor of the Union Missionary Baptist Church , St. Petersburg Florida; Reverend Dr. Reginard Dawkins, Pastor/Org. of the Triumph Christian Center, Hampton Virginia; Reverend Curtis Johnson, pastor of the Valley Brook Church, Ware Place, S. C. and Reverend Harold Chapman, pastor of the Pine Grove AMEC, Greenwood, S. C; plus a host of other pastors, ministers, relatives and friends.

To those who assisted me in the front cover picture of the book, Mr. Greg Yon and editing, Mrs. Lashonn Edmonds, thanks so much for your cooperative spirit.

Much appreciation to all listed for your kind expressions of endorsement and support of the book; I could not have succeeded without your support and encouragement. May God bless you "real good" for your spirituality and generosity.

The Purpose of Book

This book was written from personal experience, biblical exegesis, social and psychological data to fulfill every requirement necessary to remove all doubt and excuse of the necessity for fathers to maintain healthy relationships with their children. The hope and prayer of the writer is to categorically convince every father that if he loves his children (as he says), he cannot, for any reason desert them in hope that somehow miraculously they will live happy and proficient lives.

Every day, the statistics stand up both screaming and shouting facts to the contrary. Example: "Confused identities. Boys who grow up in father-absent homes are more likely than those in father-present homes to have trouble establishing appropriate sex roles and gender identity" (P.L. Adams, J.R. Milner, and N.A. Schrepf, Fatherless Children, New York, Wiley Press, 1984).

This is just one pebble of dysfunction among the mountainous examples awaiting children of absentee fathers. Further, note the statistics cited at the end of this chapter. Fathers, love your children and do not gamble with their destiny. Paul said, "Fathers, do not exasperate your children; instead, bring them up in the training and instruction of the Lord" (Eph. 6:4, NIV).

While the book focuses mainly on the father, it was written also for the benefit of the entire family. It needs reading by women and children with the hope and prayer that they, too, will gain the knowledge and strength necessary to properly assess the men that they choose to be in their lives.

Additionally, as crucial as it is for fathers to know their importance in the lives of their children, it is just as crucial for women to know the importance of the father's presence in the lives of their children. Hopefully, this knowledge will assist both the man and the woman to withstand more in maintaining the family's unity and integrity. This book is a must read for people that hold family values at the peak of the totem pole of importance.

Finally, the author not only concedes the fact that there are successful men and women who did not have the presence or support of their father, but also congratulates them and their mothers for a job extremely well done. In no way, shape, or form, does this book diminish the wonderful work of women heading their households (the author himself is a product of one).

The book was written to inform and motivate men to man up and accept their responsibility. Also, it substantiates many reasons why fathers must remain in relationship with their children. Notice, it was not said fathers should give child support and other physical items, although clearly they should, but giving their children a loving and nurturing relationship is far more needed. If for other reasons, fathers do it for the children's sake and obedience to God. God's Word says, "If anyone does not provide for his relatives and especially, the members of his household; he has denied the faith and is worse than an unbeliever" (I Tim. 5: 8, NIV).

Chapter I
Introduction

It must never be forgotten that the most important building block of any society is the family. Any serious study of history will validate the claim. To its importance, please note that out of the many manmade institutions, the only two institutions created by God both concern the family: the family of man, and the family of God, the body of baptized believers in Christ Jesus. The only reasonable conclusion that can be drawn from this creative phenomenon of God is, to Him, the family is top priority and the foundation and cornerstone of mankind's existence.

In such a topsy-turvy world of turmoil and uncertainty, it is more important than ever for man, as did God to make the family the center and top priority of his existence. Without debate, let it be proudly proclaimed, families are the core relationship in the heavenly Father's plan.

Although times reflect the changing of man's morality as repeatedly indicated in the U.S. Census Bureau's findings. It reports, on the escalator of human relationships, marriage is declining and divorce inclining.

The transformative trends of the past fifty years that led to a sharp decline in marriage and a rise of new family forms were shaped by attitudes and behaviors that differ by class, age, and race. This is according to a new Pew Research Center nationwide survey, conducted in association with *TIME* magazine, and complemented by an analysis of demographic and economic data from the U.S. Census Bureau.

Example: The divorce rate in America for first marriage versus second or third marriages.

Fifty percent of first marriages, 67 percent of second and 74 percent of third marriages end in divorce, according to Jennifer

Baker of the Forest Institute of Professional Psychology in Springfield, Missouri.

The statistics reveal an important reality. After the first marriage, the success rate diminishes. Here, the message is crystal clear; before marrying the first time, study long and hard. So when you stand at the altar and say, "I do," mean it, and stick to it. The Scripture and the odds of success will stand up against you the next time.

Despite the reality of the low odds of success, marriage in God's plan is still ordered for society's health and wellbeing. In marriage, the husband and wife have a solemn responsibility to love and care for each other and for their children. "Children are a heritage of the Lord" (Psalms 127:3).

Parents have a sacred duty to rear their children in love and righteousness, to provide for their physical and spiritual needs, to teach them to love and serve one another, to observe the commandments of God and to be law-abiding citizens wherever they live.

Husbands and wives—mothers and fathers—will be held accountable before God for the discharge of these obligations. Proverbs 22:6, says, "Train a child in the way he should go, and when he is old he will not depart from it."

It is a fact of life that the social order of society already recognizes and is seen in the dispensation of the rules of operation for citizens of the United States of America. In the Declaration of Independence, the founding fathers of this country not only stated, but also declared the rights of the family and the individual.

The Declaration of Independence declares, "We hold these truths to be self-evident, that all men are created equal that they are endowed by their Creator with certain unalienable Rights; that among these are Life, Liberty and the pursuit of Happiness. To secure these rights, Governments are instituted among Men, deriving their just powers from the consent of the governed."

One of the intentions of this book is to show that the welfare of the children of the United States was included in the Declaration of Independence. That they too are equal and have been endowed by their Creator with certain unalienable rights, that among these are life, liberty, and the pursuit of happiness.

Thus, America and the world must not forget the children. They have been endowed with certain unalienable rights for options and opportunities to improve themselves and pursue life, liberty, and happiness. It needs specifically noting that these rights declared by the founding fathers does not depend upon race, religion, creed and color or the side of the tracks on which children happen to be born.

Inherent by both God and the founding fathers, each child is somebody special and deserves to be treated with dignity and respect. On the subject, note the words of Jesus. "Then was brought unto him little children that he should lay hands upon them and pray: and the disciples rebuked them. But Jesus said, Suffer little children, and forbid them not, to come unto me: for of such is the kingdom of heaven." And he laid his hands on them, and departed thence (Matt. 19: 13-15 KJV).

Also note Matt. 18:6, "Jesus said, "But whoso shall offend one of these little ones which believe in me, it were better for him that a millstone were hanged about his neck, and that he was drowned in the depth of the sea" (Matt. 18: 6 KJV).

It is a fair assessment of the book to say, it is a family-oriented writing with emphasis on the father, but also on the mother and children and their roles in society. It submits the role of the father to be the key one played in the drama of the children lives. If fathers do not play the master key role, still it is one of the two major ones played out on the stage of family life. Of course, the mother is the other.

Unfortunately today, society has significantly reduced the role of father, specifically in the areas of provider and authority. In the Epistle to the Church at Ephesus, Paul addressed the family structure issue. He writes: "Wives, submit to your own husbands, as to the Master. For the husband is head of the wife, as also Christ is head of the Assembly; and He is the Savior of the body. As the Assembly is subject to Christ, so let the wives be to their own husbands in everything. Husbands, love your wives, just as Christ loved the assembly and gave Himself for her" (Eph. 5: 22-25).

In today's politically correct-driven climate, society as a whole refuses to accept the husband's role of authority within the family structure. This is not only disrespectful and demeaning to the father, but also to the family and the Word of God. Paul says, "The wife is to submit to her husband as to Christ. Thus, as the assembly is to obey Christ, the wife likewise should also obey her husband in the Lord." The Scripture submits the father with the final authority within the family structure.

This authority was also placed on the stage and played out in the drama of creation. God makes no mistakes, and thus man's physical gifts of protector and authority were not given accidentally. For instance, at 3:00 a.m. when there is a scratch on the windowsill, there is no argument of authority taking place between the wife and husband about who will go out into the dark and investigate the possible danger. Automatically, the assumption is that the husband will take the risk because he is the protector of the family and rightly so.

Additionally Paul said the husband is to love his wife as Christ loved the assembly. It is important to note that our Savior, Christ, and Messiah never abused his authority over the assembly. In the same manner, Paul admonished the husband to never use his God-given authority to abuse his wife or family. The husband is to love his wife and family as Christ loved the Church" (Eph. 5).

The father of the children or husband living in the home is not to provoke the children. It has been brought to the attention of many family promoters that some men intentionally provoke their children. This is more than shameful; it is a serious violation of the Word of God and God's trust to the man as head and leader.

Note: the first three verses of Ephesians 6 are directed toward children and tells them to "obey your parents" and "honor your father and mother." Then the spotlight shifts from children to fathers and says, "Fathers, provoke not your children to wrath" (Ephesians 6:4). Colossians 3:21 reads similarly: "Fathers, provoke not your children to anger, lest they be discouraged."

Anger and *wrath*—these are devastating emotions in children and young people. Fathers, mothers, or others who have the oversight of children should understand the long-term ramifications of sustained anger in children. The Apostle Paul was well aware that Roman fathers had the freedom to treat their children in any way they chose. So he directs them to not provoke, but love their children.

As most parents are well aware, there is a difference between discipline, destructive criticism, and provocation. There is no doubt that children need reproof and correction. Identifying behavioral boundaries and insisting that children stay within them is the natural duty of parents. But insulting, destructive criticism that implies stupidity on the part of children is emotionally destructive.

The Apostle Peter wrote, "And above all things have fervent love for one another, for love will cover a multitude of sins" (I Peter 4:8). In other words, loving parents will not constantly remind their children of past failures or sins and certainly will not provoke them for pleasure. They must love their children and forgive and forget.

Over the years, there have been many studies published on the necessity of fathers in the lives of their children. It's sad to say, as of today's date, the majority of men have not received (or should I say accepted) the message.

It needs emphasizing more frequent, more loud and clear that without a father, a child is much more likely to engage in abusive, harmful, undisciplined, and unproductive behavior. In an article entitled "The Plight of Fatherless Children" from Gazette.net, the following discoveries were noted of children without active fathers in their lives:

- Sixty-three percent of young people who commit suicide are from fatherless homes.
- Eighty-five percent of children who exhibit behavioral disorders are from fatherless homes.
- Eighty percent of rapists are from fatherless homes.
- Seventy-one percent of high school dropouts are from fatherless homes.
- Seventy-five percent of all adolescent patients in chemical-abuse centers are from fatherless homes.
- Seventy percent of juveniles in state operated institutions come from fatherless homes.
- Eighty-five percent of youth in prison are from fatherless homes.
- Seventy percent of pregnant teens are from fatherless homes.

The statistics are simply astounding. Knowledge of them is certainly enough motivation for any father to take a second, even third or fourth look at the family situation before dismissing himself. The devastating information reflects the majority of studies documenting the impact of fatherless homes. There is one recurring theme; without the presence of strong fathers, children pay the price and suffer in many profound ways.

The omniscience of the Creator is reflected in the studies. In that, when God created man and woman and brought them together, His knowledge and fore plan for the family unit was revealed. After which, He told them to be fruitful and multiply and replenish the earth" (Genesis 1: 28 KJV). The fruit of the family unit will sustain the generations.

Without the establishment and installation of this core unit, no culture has a remote chance for long-term survival. This is a proven fact of history and with plenty substantiation.

Chapter II
The Impact of Fatherlessness On The Fatherless!

During my days as a youngster growing up in the Green Line community, these were seven of the most feared and influential words flowing; "Just wait 'til your daddy gets home!" I didn't know then as I do today that the seven words had an aspect of divine providence. With God, the number seven represents perfection and completion.

How providential, the seven words related the same sentiment in the family unit. In the hearts and minds of the children, the words ignited the urge for "perfection" and fear as the motivation for "completion."

Even today some fifty years later, I still remember the reaction of my friends when the words were spoken by their mothers (particularly the few ones with fathers residing in the home who came home on a regular basis). "Just wait 'til your daddy gets home!" Of course all biological fathers did not reside with their children. In fact, most did not back then and most do not today.

Yet, the mere utterance of the warning raised eyebrows to attention. The playful little bodies, normally relaxed and nonresponsive, immediately straightened up. It seemed that they were overcome by a new sense of obedience and respect. This reaction to the words both baffled and amazed me.

Particularly since all morning long the mothers had issued different kinds of statements, one after another warning the children to straighten up. Each warning went without reaction. The mothers said to them, "Just keep it up and see what happens." Still, no reaction. They said, "Do it one more time." Still, no reaction. They said, "You think I'm playing with you, but I'm not."

Still, no reaction. In frustration some shouted, "Did you hear me?" Still, no reaction to speak of.

At this point, a few of the mothers lost control and began to curse and swear at the children. Clearly, it was not the right thing to do, although many of the children of Green Line were rough and tough. In fact, the entire neighborhood of Green Line was rough and tough.

Even after yelling and screaming the additional threats and using what was thought to be motivational language (though inappropriate, even contradictory, because it taught the children the opposite of what was attempting to be taught), still, little or no reaction.

For this reason, it was more than amazing and startling. When the phrase was uttered, "Just wait 'til your daddy gets home," the change in behavior was drastic. Almost instantaneously, the children reacted. Their reaction was similar to that of a home experiencing a violent strike of an earthquake and the house shook to its core.

In every room, every child experienced the powerful quiver and was overcome fiercely with fear. No matter what games were being played, immediately the focus shifted, facial expression changed, and there was complete silence. All in attendance were attentive and alert.

The words, "Just wait 'til your daddy gets home" brought the same results. In shock and amazement, I slid back into the dark corners of disbelief because of the power of these seven little words.

The words were new to my ears as a newborn baby's bottom (as the old folk used to say), and I could not remember hearing them uttered ever before: at least, not in my home. In fact, I don't think the words ever crossed the lips of my mother.

(Though told later that mother did say to the older siblings, "Just wait 'til your granddaddy gets home." The influence and necessary participation of grandparents is another book waiting to be written.) Personally speaking, I don't recall Mother speaking the words.

Either way, on the face of it, using the phrase or not doesn't seem like much of an issue. In fact, it may sound like a good thing to never be told, "Just wait 'til your daddy gets home." Not to be warned and scared or intimidated into action, no matter the cause, sounds like a good thing. Not to be forced or made to do anything by threat and innuendo sounds pleasing, at least on the surface.

It sounds like a good thing, until you investigate the meaning behind the message. On the face of it, there are many things that sound good but are not good. Think about *ethnic cleansing* (or any kind of cleansing), sounds good until you investigate the meaning behind the message. *Friendly fire* (friendly) sounds good until you investigate the meaning behind the message. *Garnish your wages* sounds good until you investigate the meaning behind the message.

Like so it is, not to be told or intimidated with the words, "Just wait 'til your daddy gets home." It sounds good until you investigate the meaning behind the message. It sounds like a blessing, but in reality, it is a curse. It sounds positive but is negative. In the lives of many children, the absence of these words proved devastating.

Personally, I know this to be true. In my life as well as in many others that I have come into contact with, "the proof is in the pudding." The fact that the daddy of our household did not come home was disastrous. This characterization was made for a number of reasons. First, it prevented Mother from using one of the wondrous, God-given tools of correction to her children. Not to be able to say with truth and conviction, "Just wait 'til your daddy gets home" had devastating consequences.

Another sad result, at least on the face of it, to Daddy, apparently his departure was not considered important. It was not an issue and certainly not a devastating one. Apparently, his departure was not even taken seriously. As far as my siblings and I were concerned, his departure was done with too much ease. His inconsideration of the mass of potential devastation for his family was mind blowing.

Even more disturbing was his exodus without so much as a meeting with the family to at least say good-bye, see you later, or have a good life. I do not intend to be repetitive here, but fathers need to clearly understand the mental and physical struggle of the children. The repeated emphasis of the children's views must be reiterated by somebody. Their position must be presented and done so without compromise and restraint.

Fathers need to be aware of what their actions looked like in the eyes of the children. That what was done by father was desertion and was not taken lightly. How catastrophic for a man to father nine children, then walk away and never look back? How devastating for all concerned? My father is deceased now and may never know the result of his actions (except in the judgment). But his absence was devastating for all of us, as well as for him.

Fathers don't miss this!

Because Daddy wasn't there for the children, he missed out on experiencing the most wonderful blessings that life has to offer. After his desertion, maybe he had fun going southward. Maybe he owned a mansion on a hill. Maybe he ate, dressed, and drove the finest of everything in his new life. But having attained much of the above accomplishments also, I still say, he missed out on the most wonderful blessings of life. The Beatles were right, "Money can't buy me love."

He did not experience the love, affection and admiration of his children. He missed the joy and pride of seeing them accomplish great goals and fulfill their destiny. He missed hearing them express their appreciation and thanks for his sacrifice. For a father to hear and see these things, I declare, it doesn't get any better.

To Mrs. Ola Mae Henderson Lomax, my mother, my father's absence was devastation as well. It took years for her to recover.

(If she ever actually did, I cannot say). Think about it, suddenly for nine children, she was the breadwinner, teacher and protector. Imagine the burden of that fact. To better understand her predicament, think about the number of hungry mouths you are responsible to feed and the naked bodies you are responsible to clothe? How would you feel if you had nine?

Instantaneously without forewarning, mother was responsible for the total welfare of nine children plus herself. The stress and strain of that alone was tremendous and add into the equation all of the other losses. Such as the love of her life was gone and no longer was there anyone to share the Eros love with.

Moreover, father's fellowship, companionship, respect, and mutual encouragement—all gone, including the hopes and dreams they shared. Every wife and mother deserves better.

In fact, every human being deserves better. All humans deserve love, companionship, mutual respect, and encouragement. This is the will of God. In the wee hours of creation, God shared with the human family the importance of these attributes, love, fellowship, companionship, and mutual respect and encouragement. "After Adam named all of the animals, there was not found a help meet for him." Jeff A. Benner defines helpmeet:

"What does Genesis 2:18 mean when it says, "I will make him a helpmeet for him."? The Hebrew phrasing for *helpmeet* is "ezer kenegedo."

The word *ezer* means "helper." The word *neged* comes from the verbal root "nagad" meaning "to be face-to-face." This verb is always used in the causative form where it would literally be translated as "to make to be face-to-face" and means "to tell."

The noun form *neged* is often used for something that is face-to-face with something else. Such as in Genesis 21:16 where Hagar went and sat down "opposite" her son, although he was some distance away.

The prefix "ke" in the word *kenegedo* means "like" and the suffix "o" means "of him."

Putting all of this together, *ezer kenegedo* literally means "a helper like one opposite of him." This means Eve was to be his other half, like him, but with opposite attributes.

So God said, "It is not good that the man should be alone, I will create for him a help meet" (Genesis 2:18 KJV). Here, God's intentions for the human creation are heard loud and clear. In order for man to be at his best, he needs woman. For woman to be at her best, she needs man. My father's desertion deprived mother of the inherent blessings of God, love, companionship, mutual respect, and encouragement from her lifelong partner.

Unfortunately, these were not the only negatives my mother faced. Additionally, there was the unscheduled task of becoming both father and mother. Not only was the time scheduling a problem, it was a serious breach of the marriage contract.

In every marriage ceremony, there are some stated and implied terms and agreements signed and sealed by the husband and wife. For instance, in the presence of God and many witnesses, my father vowed to take my mother to be his lawful wedded wife. He vowed to love and respect her, honor and cherish her, in health and in sickness, in prosperity and in adversity; and leave all others and keep himself only unto her, so long as he lived. So mother had the right to be disheartened and disillusioned by his desertion and violation of the marital contract.

He forced her into unchartered and un-agreed to waters. Mother was now both father and mother. A task, not only unthought-of of and unprepared for was suddenly laid upon her shoulders and society full well expected her to carry the load.

The rules and regulations in place threatened her freedom if she failed: The rules of society to feed; clothed, housed and nurture the children after birth. Yet during mother's day, society made little contribution to assist in fulfilling its demands. So in many ways both society and her husband were uncaring and deserted her.

They placed her between a rock and a hard place: The defection of her husband was devastating. His actions changed her life forever. Only the best of women maintain their sanity under circumstances such as these.

The years of loneliness and stress piled up. With every year that passed, mother missed the love and affection of a companion more and more. Understandably, she had become accustomed to his presence, provision, and protection.

But now his desertion and broken promises turned mother's life upside down and inside out: A nightmarish reality that would not be easily overcome or replaced. How does one replace a father who has brought nine children into the world? How many men are willing to step in and accept this kind of responsibility of "an already made family" or if you will, a basketball squad with cheerleaders and all?

One of the associate ministers of our church often says, "When a father is misplaced, the wife is displaced and the children are all out of place." In her words, Minister Clara Carter explains her interesting position. She says, one may ask, what does she mean by the above statement? First of all, man was given charge over the woman as protector and provider, so, what happened?

After the sin and God appearance in the Garden for correction, Adam blamed God for giving him the gift of woman. Yet, in reality, God's gift was in his best interest. Remember, God said, "It was not good for man to be alone, so God created for him a helpmeet."

The question is, where was Adam when the deceiver came? Eve was left unprotected. Where was Adam spiritually, although standing at her side, physically, he was not minding the sheep and protecting the camp? Also, remember, Abraham told Sarah to lie and say, "You are my sister." He figured her lie would save his life.

Adam put the woman in harm's way. That is disappointment with man; he often leaves the woman vulnerable and unprotected. She was not created to fend for herself. Today still, women seriously struggle because of the man's absence. Many are alone; yet, still have the responsibility of taking care of themselves and the children.

So guess what, because of man's desertion, the woman has to leave her post unguarded, go out into unchartered waters, and bring the bread and bacon home. "Against the wiles of the devil," the children also are vulnerable, left alone at home to fend for themselves.

The question needs repeating, who is minding the camp? Children left without guidance, to wander aimlessly into all sorts of mischief. They go to and fro, from one friend's house to the next without parental permission or knowledge. With so much freedom to roam, it's no wonder there's so much promiscuity. Who is minding the camp?

Many daddies deserted the family, moms at work and only God knows where the children are. The world needs to return to the days of Walter Cronkite. During the late sixties and early seventies, at the close of his news broadcast, he would say, "It's eleven o'clock, do you know where your children are?" Back in the day, the roles of the family were better defined. Each entity—father, mother, and child—understood both the beginning and the ending of their roles.

Today things are different, which somewhat may help explain the reason there are so many women confused and lost. Many are lost and maybe their lost-ness caused them to think crazy and unnatural thoughts.

Also, many women are misunderstood by men. So much so that many believe the only people that understand them are other women—thus leading to lesbianism and bisexual activity. How deceptive and sad is the devil's handiwork. It's just another example of the misguidance of the enemy. Once again, I reference the deception that occurred in the Garden of Eden. How awful and tragic!

Example: note the dilemma of first woman. Adam was around, but his operation as the man of protection failed miserably. He did not offer any resistance to the eating of the forbidden fruit. Think about it; if he had protected her, the enemy (the deceiver, serpent, devil) would not have convinced her to disobey God. What disaster his silence caused the world. Adam should have spoken up and defended her and God.

Eve did not know the commands like Adam. The Bible does not indicate her presence at the distribution of the God's law, only Adam. Thus, God gave the commands to the man. Adam was the recipient, and for an unknown amount of time, he was there alone before Eve's arrival. Although it must be stated and made known, emphatically that Adam told Eve what God's commands were because she quoted many of them to the serpent.

Allow me the privilege to ask man another question, how can the woman be what she needs and was created to be without the man? Remember, she was created to stand by his side, to be his helpmeet. Seriously, men need to examine their roles in order to regain their rightful place with God and mankind.

Although women have to answer to the Creator as well, still, it was man who was given the charge of protection for the family. Think about it, men, wake up and return to the camp and finish what God started.

Here's another sad plight of women. They have to raise boys to be men. What a challenge for women. Men are absent, and women are left to raise boys. It is no wonder that there are so many boys exemplifying female tendencies like their mothers. The business of becoming both parents has placed tremendous stress and strain on mothers. So much so, that many times women get confused as to who or what they are.

In some instances, mothers must become masculine for doing chores around the house, etc. In other instances, she must be feminine and teach her daughters femininity. It must grieve the Almighty God to see what is happening to his creation. However, God deserves the glory and thanksgiving for sending us Jesus! He made a way to redeem us.

Can you imagine for a moment what the family of mankind would be like if the man was in place, the woman not displaced, and the children not all over the place? There is a good chance that they would be still playing and having inexhaustible fun in their own backyards in the Garden of Eden. God's will would be done, and the father's role as a loving, providing, and protector, keeping the wife and children in place would give the devil fits.

It is a divine mandate of God for all of the family members to be in place. Man first, woman second (standing at his side, after all, she was taken from a rib in his side) and the children under subjection. The family should resemble the Trinity (Father, Son and Holy Ghost) having three distinctions but the same spirit of unity.

People of God need to return to the Creator's rule and divine orders. Through prayer and supplication, men, women, and children need to seek their role. Jesus said to the church at Ephesus, repent and return to thou first love (Rev. 2: 4-5 KJV). If mankind would return to their first love, things will fall back in order, despite how crazy everything looks. Amen.

To Minister Carter's observations and assessment, I am happy to say *Amen*: particularly because I grew up a fatherless child. As such, I can speak for fatherless children. More specifically, being the youngest of nine fatherless children, I can testify personally of the devastation that a father's (or a mother's) absence plays in the life of their children. At the age of three (so I was told by mother, brothers and sisters) our father left me, my mother, five brothers and three sisters.

Fathers, listen up! I'm sick and tired of seeing the children sick and tired!

Every child born deserves the privilege of knowing and experiencing love from both their father and mother. In fact, it is an unalienable right that every child should have wonderful memories of care and nurture. To deprive them of this is almost blasphemous and surely unconstitutional. On the pages of the U.S. Constitution, it is so stated:

"There is a fundamental liberty and right guaranteed to the family by the 14th Amendment. This is the right to the care, custody, and nurture of their children. According to the Supreme Court of the United States: 'Absent a Compelling State Interest of harm or potential harm to the child, the State may not intervene in the privacy of family life.'"

While the U.S. States Constitution gives parents the rights of care, custody, and nurture of their children, the Declaration of Independence gives the children (as all human beings) the right to pursue life, liberty, and happiness. Thus, parenthood must be taken seriously, socially, spiritually, and legally. In fact, even the sacrifices of parenthood must be considered seriously by every potential parent before mentally entertaining the thought of conceiving children.

However, like billions of other children across the nation and world, I grew up with great support from my mother. On the other hand, from my father, there was little or no support. His absence and lack of involvement resulted in serious dysfunctions. I am a living witness and testifier to the truth of many of the following statistics from Dads4kids.com: Fathers, pay close attention!

Statistics of a Fatherless America:

Make note of the infamous fatherless children at the bottom of the article!

"Sexual activity: In a study of 700 adolescents, researchers found that "compared to families with two natural parents living in the home, adolescents from single-parent families have been found to engage in greater and earlier sexual activity." Source: Carol W. Metzler, et al. "The Social Context for Risky Sexual Behavior Among Adolescents," Journal of Behavioral Medicine 17 (1994).

A myriad of maladies: Fatherless children are at a dramatically greater risk of drug and alcohol abuse, mental illness, suicide, poor educational performance, teen pregnancy, and criminality. Source: U.S. Department of Health and Human Services,

National Center for Health Statistics, Survey on Child Health, Washington, DC, 1993.

Drinking problems: Teenagers living in single-parent households are more likely to abuse alcohol and at an earlier age compared to children reared in two-parent households Source: Terry E. Duncan, Susan C. Duncan and Hyman Hops, "The Effects of Family Cohesiveness and Peer Encouragement on the Development of Adolescent Alcohol Use: A Cohort-Sequential Approach to the Analysis of Longitudinal Data," Journal of Studies on Alcohol 55 (1994).

Drug Use: "...the absence of the father in the home affects significantly the behavior of adolescents and results in the greater use of alcohol and marijuana." Source: Deane Scott Berman, "Risk Factors Leading to Adolescent Substance Abuse," Adolescence 30 (1995)

Sexual abuse: A study of 156 victims of child sexual abuse found that the majority of the children came from disrupted or single-parent homes; only 31 percent of the children lived with both biological parents. Although stepfamilies make up only about 10 percent of all families, 27 percent of the abused children lived with either a stepfather or the mother's boyfriend. Source: Beverly Gomes-Schwartz, Jonathan Horowitz, and Albert P. Cardarelli, "Child Sexual Abuse Victims and Their Treatment," U.S. Department of Justice, Office of Juvenile Justice and Delinquency Prevention.

Child Abuse: Researchers in Michigan determined that "49 percent of all child abuse cases are committed by single mothers." Source: Joan Ditson and Sharon Shay, "A Study of Child Abuse in Lansing, Michigan," Child Abuse and Neglect, 8 (1984).

Deadly predictions: A family structure index—a composite index based on the annual rate of children involved in divorce and the percentage of families with children present that are female-headed—is a strong predictor of suicide among young adult and adolescent white males. Source: Patricia L. McCall and Kenneth

C. Land, "Trends in White Male Adolescent, Young-Adult and Elderly Suicide: Are There Common Underlying Structural Factors?" Social Science Research 23, 1994.

High risk: Fatherless children are at dramatically greater risk of suicide. Source: U.S. Department of Health and Human Services, National Center for Health Statistics, Survey on Child Health, Washington, DC, 1993.

Suicidal Tendencies: In a study of 146 adolescent friends of twenty-six adolescent suicide victims, teens living in single-parent families are not only more likely to commit suicide but also more likely to suffer from psychological disorders, when compared to teens living in intact families. Source: David A. Brent, et al. "Post-traumatic Stress Disorder in Peers of Adolescent Suicide Victims: Predisposing Factors and Phenomenology." Journal of the American Academy of Child and Adolescent Psychiatry 34, 1995.

Confused identities: Boys who grow up in father-absent homes are more likely that those in father-present homes to have trouble establishing appropriate sex roles and gender identity. Source: P.L. Adams, J.R. Milner, and N.A. Schrepf, Fatherless Children, New York, Wiley Press, 1984.

Psychiatric Problems: In 1988, a study of preschool children admitted to New Orleans hospitals as psychiatric patients over a thirty-four-month period found that nearly 80 percent came from fatherless homes. Source: Jack Block, et al. "Parental Functioning and the Home Environment in Families of Divorce," Journal of the American Academy of Child and Adolescent Psychiatry, 27 (1988)

Emotional distress: Children living with a never-married mother are more likely to have been treated for emotional problems. Source: L. Remez, "Children Who Don't Live with Both Parents Face Behavioral Problems," Family Planning Perspectives (January/February 1992).

Uncooperative kids: Children reared by a divorced or never-married mother are less cooperative and score lower on tests of intelligence than children reared in intact families. Statistical analysis of the behavior and intelligence of these children revealed "significant detrimental effects" of living in a female-headed household. Growing up in a female-headed household remained a statistical predictor of behavior problems even after adjusting for differences in family income. Source: Greg L. Duncan, Jeanne Brooks-Gunn and Pamela Kato Klebanov, "Economic Deprivation and Early Childhood Development," Child Development 65 (1994).

Unstable families, unstable lives: Compared to peers in two-parent homes, children in single-parent households are more likely to engage in troublesome behavior, and perform poorly in school. Source: Tom Luster and Hariette Pipes McAdoo, "Factors Related to the Achievement and Adjustment of Young African-American Children." Child Development 65 (1994): 1080-1094

Beyond class lines: Even controlling for variations across groups in parent education, race and other child and family factors, eighteen- to twenty-two-year-olds from disrupted families were twice as likely to have poor relationships with their mothers and fathers, to show high levels of emotional distress or problem behavior, [and] to have received psychological help. Source: Nicholas Zill, Donna Morrison, and Mary Jo Coiro, "Long Term Effects of Parental Divorce on Parent-Child Relationships, Adjustment and Achievement in Young Adulthood." Journal of Family Psychology 7 (1993).

Fatherly influence: Children with fathers at home tend to do better in school, are less prone to depression and are more successful in relationships. Children from one-parent families achieve less and get into trouble more than children from two parent families. Source: One Parent Families and Their Children: The School's Most Significant Minority, conducted by The Consortium for the Study of School Needs of Children from One Parent Families, cosponsored by the National Association of Elementary School Principals and the Institute for Development of Educational Activities, a division of the Charles F. Kettering Foundation, Arlington, VA., 1980.

Divorce disorders: Children whose parents separate are significantly more likely to engage in early sexual activity, abuse drugs, and experience conduct and mood disorders. This effect is especially strong for children whose parents separated when they were five years old or younger. Source: David M. Fergusson, John Horwood and Michael T. Lynsky, "Parental Separation, Adolescent Psychopathology, and Problem Behaviors," Journal of the American Academy of Child and Adolescent Psychiatry 33 (1944).

Troubled marriages, troubled kids: Compared to peers living with both biological parents, sons and daughters of divorced or separated parents exhibited significantly more conduct problems. Daughters of divorced or separated mothers evidenced significantly higher rates of internalizing problems, such as anxiety or depression. Source: Denise B. Kandel, Emily Rosenbaum and Kevin Chen, "Impact of Maternal Drug Use and Life Experiences on Preadolescent Children Born to Teenage Mothers," Journal of Marriage and the Family56 (1994).

Hungry for love: "Father hunger" often afflicts boys age one and two whose fathers are suddenly and permanently absent. Sleep disturbances, such as trouble falling asleep, nightmares, and night terrors frequently begin within one to three months after the father leaves home. Source: Alfred A. Messer, "Boys Father Hunger: The Missing Father Syndrome," Medical Aspects of Human Sexuality, January 1989.

Disturbing news: Children of never-married mothers are more than twice as likely to have been treated for an emotional or behavioral problem. Source: U.S. Department of Health and Human Services, National Center for Health Statistics, National Health Interview Survey, Hyattsille, MD, 1988

Poor and in trouble: A 1988 Department of Health and Human Services study found that at every income level except the very highest (over $50,000 a year), children living with never-married mothers were more likely than their counterparts in two-parent families to have been expelled or suspended from school, to display emotional problems, and to engage in antisocial behavior. Source: James Q. Wilson, "In Loco Parentis: Helping Children When Families Fail Them," The Brookings Review, Fall 1993.

Fatherless aggression: In a longitudinal study of 1,197 fourth-grade students, researchers observed "greater levels of aggression in boys from mother-only households than from boys in mother-father households." Source: N. Vaden-Kierman, N. Ialongo, J. Pearson, and S. Kellam, "Household Family Structure and Children's Aggressive Behavior: A Longitudinal Study of Urban Elementary School Children," Journal of Abnormal Child Psychology 23, no. 5 (1995).

Act now, pay later: "Children from mother-only families have less of an ability to delay gratification and poorer impulse control (that is, control over anger and sexual gratification.) These children also have a weaker sense of conscience or sense of right and wrong." Source: E.M. Hetherington and B. Martin, "Family Interaction" in H.C. Quay and J.S. Werry (eds.), Psychopathological Disorders of Childhood. (New York: John Wiley & Sons, 1979)

Crazy victims: Eighty percent of adolescents in psychiatric hospitals come from broken homes. Source: J.B. Elshtain, "Family Matters...", Christian Century, July 1993.

Duh to dead: "The economic consequences of a [father's] absence are often accompanied by psychological consequences, which include higher-than-average levels of youth suicide, low intellectual and education performance, and higher-than-average rates of mental illness, violence and drug use." Source: William Galston, Elaine Kamarck. Progressive Policy Institute. 1993

Expelled: Nationally, 15.3 percent of children living with a never-married mother and 10.7 percent of children living with a divorced mother have been expelled or suspended from school, compared to only 4.4 percent of children living with both biological parents. Source: Debra Dawson, "Family Structure...", Journal of Marriage and Family, No. 53. 1991.

Violent rejection: Kids who exhibited violent behavior at school were 11 times as likely not to live with their fathers and six times as likely to have parents who were not married. Boys from families with absent fathers are at higher risk for violent behavior than boys from intact families. Source: J.L. Sheline (et al.), "Risk Factors...", American Journal of Public Health, No. 84. 1994.

That crowd: Children without fathers or with stepfathers were less likely to have friends who think it's important to behave properly in school. They also exhibit more problems with behavior and in achieving goals. Source: Nicholas Zill, C. W. Nord, "Running in Place," Child Trends, Inc. 1994.

Likeliest to succeed: Kids who live with both biological parents at age 14 are significantly more likely to graduate from high school than those kids who live with a single parent, a parent and step-parent, or neither parent. Source: G.D. Sandefur (et al.), "The Effects of Parental Marital Status...", Social Forces, September 1992.

Worse to bad: Children in single-parent families tend to score lower on standardized tests and to receive lower grades in school. Children in single-parent families are nearly twice as likely to drop out of school as children from two-parent families. Source: J.B. Stedman (et al.), "Dropping Out," Congressional Research Service Report No 88-417. 1988.

College odds: Children from disrupted families are 20 percent more unlikely to attend college than kids from intact, two-parent families. Source: J. Wallerstein, Family Law Quarterly, 20. (Summer 1986)

On their own: Kids living in single-parent homes or in step-families report lower educational expectations on the part of their parents, less parental monitoring of school work, and less overall social supervision than children from intact families. Source: N.M. Astore and S. McLanahan, Americican Sociological Review, No. 56 (1991)

Double-risk: Fatherless children—kids living in homes without a stepfather or without contact with their biological father—are twice as likely to drop out of school. Source: U.S. Dept. of Health and Human Services, Survey on Child Health. (1993)

Repeat, repeat: Nationally, 29.7 percent of children living with a never-married mother and 21.5 percent of children living with a divorced mother have repeated at least one grade in school, compared to 11.6 percent of children living with both biological parents. Source: Debra Dawson, "Family Structure and Children's Well-Being," Journals of Marriage and Family, No. 53. (1991).

Underpaid high achievers: Children from low-income, two-parent families outperform students from high-income, single-parent homes. Almost twice as many high achievers come from two-parent homes as one-parent homes. Source: "One-Parent Families and Their Children;" Charles F. Kettering Foundation (1990).

Dadless and dumb: At least one-third of children experiencing a parental separation "demonstrated a significant decline in academic performance" persisting at least three years. Source: L.M.C. Bisnairs (et al.), American Journal of Orthopsychiatry, No. 60 (1990)

Son of Solo: According to a recent study of young, non-custodial fathers who are behind on child support payments, less than half of these men were living with their own father at age 14.

Slip-sliding: Among black children between the ages of six to nine years old, black children in mother-only households scored significantly lower on tests of intellectual ability, than black children living with two parents. Source: Luster and McAdoo, Child Development 65. 1994.

Dadless dropouts: After taking into account race, socio-economic status, sex, age and ability, high school students from single-parent households were 1.7 times more likely to drop out than were their corresponding counterparts living with both biological parents.Source: Ralph McNeal, Sociology of Education 88. 1995.

Takes two: Families in which both the child's biological or adoptive parents are present in the household show significantly higher levels of parental involvement in the child's school activities than do mother-only families or step-families. Source: Zill and Nord, "Running in Place." Child Trends. 1994.

Con garden: Forty-three percent of prison inmates grew up in a single-parent household—39 percent with their mothers, 4 percent with their fathers—and an additional 14 percent lived in households without either biological parent. Another 14 percent had spent at last part of their childhood in a foster home, agency or other juvenile institution. Source: US Bureau of Justice Statistics, Survey of State Prison Inmates. 1991.

Criminal moms, criminal kids: The children of single teenage mothers are more at risk for later criminal behavior. In the case of a teenage mother, the absence of a father also increases the risk of harshness from the mother. Source: M. Mourash, L. Rucker, Crime and Delinquency 35,1989.

Rearing rapists: Seventy-two percent of adolescent murderers grew up without fathers. Sixty percent of America's rapists grew up the same way. Source: D. Cornell (et al.), Behavioral Sciences and the Law, 5. 1987. And N. Davidson, "Life without Father," Policy Review. 1990.

Crime and poverty: The proportion of single-parent households in a community predicts its rate of violent crime and burglary, but the community's poverty level does not. Source: D.A. Smith and G.R. Jarjoura, "Social Structure and Criminal Victimization," Journal of Research in Crime and Delinquency 25. 1988.

Marriage matters: Only 13 percent of juvenile delinquents come from families in which the biological mother and father are married to each other. By contrast, 33 percent have parents who are either divorced or separated and 44 percent have parents who were never married. Source: Wisconsin Dept. of Health and Social Services, April 1994.

No good time: Compared to boys from intact, two-parent families, teenage boys from disrupted families are not only more likely to be incarcerated for delinquent offenses, but also to manifest worse conduct while incarcerated. Source: M Eileen Matlock et al., "Family Correlates of Social Skills..." Adolescence 29. 1994.

Count them: Seventy percent of juveniles in state reform institutions grew up in single- or no-parent situations. Source: Alan Beck et al., Survey of Youth in Custody, 1987, US Bureau of Justice Statistics, 1988.

The Main Thing: The relationship between family structure and crime is so strong that controlling for family configuration erases the relationship between race and crime and between low income and crime. This conclusion shows up time and again in the literature. Source: E. Kamarck, William Galston, Putting Children First, Progressive Policy Inst. 1990

Examples: Teenage fathers are more likely than their childless peers to commit and be convicted of illegal activity, and their offenses are of a more serious nature. Source: M.A. Pirog-Good, "Teen Father and the Child Support System," in Paternity Establishment, Institute for research on Poverty, Univ.

The 'hood:' The likelihood that a young male will engage in criminal activity doubles if he is raised without a father and triples if he lives in a neighborhood with a high concentration of single-parent families. Source: A. Anne Hill, June O'Neill, "Underclass Behaviors in the United States," CUNY, Baruch College. 1993

I grew up in the hood and personally testify that I engaged in criminal activities as a young lad. The majority of my friends did not have fathers directly involved in their lives and they were involved in criminal activities as well. At the age of nine, I ran the streets way past midnight committing acts that are too embarrassing and illegal to discuss. I will say that I escaped serious injury, death and jail only by the grace of God. Parents and caretakers know where your children are. They are not as innocent or ignorant to Satan's devices as you may think.

Bringing the war back home: The odds that a boy born in America in 1974 will be murdered are higher than the odds that a serviceman in World War II would be killed in combat. Source: US Sen. Phil Gramm, 1995

Get ahead at home and at work: Fathers who cared for their children intellectual development and their adolescent's social development were more like to advance in their careers, compared to men who weren't involved in such activities. Source: J. Snarey, How Fathers Care for the Next Generation. Harvard Univ. Press.

Diaper dads: In 1991, about 20 percent of preschool children were cared for by their fathers—both married and single. In 1988, the number was 15 percent. Source: M. O'Connell, "Where's Papa? Father's Role in Child Care," Population Reference Bureau. 1993.

Without leave: Sixty-three percent of 1500 CEOs and human resource directors said it was not reasonable for a father to take a leave after the birth of a child. Source: J.H. Pleck, "Family Supportive Employer Policies," Center for research in Women. 1991.

Get a job: The number of men who complain that work conflicts with their family responsibilities rose from 12 percent in 1977 to 72 percent in 1989. Meanwhile, 74 percent of men prefer a "daddy track" job to a "fast track" job. Source: James Levine, The Fatherhood Project.

Long-distance dads: Twenty-six percent of absent fathers live in a different state than their children. Source: U.S. Bureau of the Census, Statistical Brief. 1991.

Cool Dad of the Week: Among fathers who maintain contact with their children after a divorce, the pattern of the relationship between father-and-child changes. They begin to behave more like relatives than like parents. Instead of helping with homework, nonresident dads are more likely to take the kids shopping, to the movies, or out to dinner. Instead of providing steady advice and guidance, divorced fathers become "treat dads." Source: F. Furstenberg, A. Cherlin, Divided Families . Harvard Univ. Press. 1991.

Older not wiser: While 57 percent of unwed dads with kids no older than two visit their children more than once a week, by the time the kid's seven and a half, only 23 percent are in frequent contact with their children. Source: R. Lerman and Theodora Ooms, Young Unwed Fathers. 1993.

Ten years after: Ten years after the breakup of a marriage, more than two-thirds of kids report not having seen their father for a year. Source: National Commission on Children, Speaking of Kids. 1991.

No such address: More than half the kids who don't live with their father have never been in their father's house. Source: F. Furstenberg, A. Cherlin, Divided Families. Harvard Univ. Press. 1991.

Dadless years: About 40 percent of the kids living in fatherless homes haven't seen their dads in a year or more. Of the rest, only one in five sleeps even one night a month at the father's home. And only one in six sees their father once or more per week. Source: F. Furstenberg, A. Cherlin, Divided Families. Harvard Univ. Press. 1991.

Measuring up? According to a 1992 Gallup poll, more than 50 percent of all adults agreed that fathers today spend less time with their kids than their fathers did with them. Source: Gallup national random sample conducted for the National Center for Fathering, April 1992.

Father unknown. Of kids living in single-mom households, 35 percent never see their fathers, and another 24 percent see their fathers less than once a month. Source: J.A. Selzer, "Children's Contact with Absent Parents," Journal of Marriage and the Family, 50 (1988).

Missed contact: In a study of 304 young adults, those whose parents divorced after they left home had significantly less contact with their fathers than adult children who parents remained married. Weekly contact with their children dropped from 78 percent for still-married fathers to 44 percent for divorced fathers. Source: William Aquilino, "Later Life Parental Divorce and Widowhood," Journal of Marriage and the Family 56. 1994.

Commercial breaks: The amount of time a father spends with his child—one-on-one—averages less than ten minutes a day. Source: J. P. Robinson, et al., "The Rhythm of Everyday Life." Westview Press. 1988

High risk: Overall, more than 75 percent of American children are at risk because of paternal deprivation. Even in two-parent homes, fewer than 25 percent of young boys and girls experience an average of at least one hour a day of relatively individualized contact with their fathers. Source: Henry Biller, "The Father Factor..." a paper based on presentations during meetings with William Galston, Deputy Director, Domestic Policy, Clinton White House, December 1993 and April 1994.

Knock, knock: Of children age five to fourteen, 1.6 million return home to houses where there is no adult present. Source: U.S. Bureau of the Census, "Who's Minding the Kids?" Statistical Brief. April 1994.

Who said talk's cheap? Almost 20 percent of sixth- through twelfth-graders have not had a good conversation lasting for at least ten minutes with at least one of their parents in more than a month. Source: Peter Benson, "The Troubled Journey." Search Institute. 1993.

Justified guilt: A 1990 L.A. Times poll found that 57 percent of all fathers and 55 percent of all mothers feel guilty about not spending enough time with their children. Source: Lynn Smith and Bob Sipchen, "Two Career Family Dilemma," Los Angeles Times, Aug. 12, 1990.

Who are you, mister? In 1965, parents on average spent approximately thirty hours a week with their kids. By 1985, the amount of time had fallen to seventeen hours. Source: William Mattox, "The Parent Trap." Policy Review. Winter, 1991.

Waiting Works: Only eight percent of those who finished high school, got married before having a child, and waited until age 20 to have that child were living in poverty in 1992. Source: William Galston, "Beyond the Murphy Brown Debate." Institute for Family Values. Dec. 10, 1993.

As demonstrated the father's absence was devastation to high percentages of children, which substantiates the need for writing the book. Again, make note that this book was written from personal experience, biblical exegesis and social and psychological data to fulfill every requirement necessary to remove all doubt and excuse of the necessity for fathers to maintain healthy relationships with their children.

The hope and prayer of the writer is to categorically convince every father that if he loves his children (as he says), he cannot for any reason desert them in hope that somehow miraculously they will live happy and proficient lives.

Every day the statistics stand up screaming and shouting facts to the contrary. Example: Confused identities. Boys who grow up in father-absent homes are more likely than those in father-present homes to have trouble establishing appropriate sex roles and gender identity. Source: P.L. Adams, J.R. Milner, and N.A. Schrepf, Fatherless Children, New York, Wiley Press, 1984. Fathers that love their children will not gamble with their destiny. Fathers, ask yourselves, how much do you really love your children?

Jesus asked Peter three times, "Do you love me? Peter assured Jesus that he loved him. Jesus said, "If you love me, feed my sheep" (John 21: 15-17 KJV). Jesus's understanding of love consists of demonstration: "Actions speaks louder than words", "Talk is cheap, it takes money to buy land", "But be you doers of the word, and not hearers only, deceiving your own selves" (James 1: 23 KJV).

Additionally, James asks the question, "What does it profit, my brethren, if someone says he has faith but does not have works? Can faith save him? If a brother or sister is naked and destitute of daily food and one of you says to them, "Depart in peace, be warmed and filled," but you do not give them the things which are needed for the body, what does it profit? Thus also faith by itself, if it does not have works, is dead.

But someone will say, "You have faith, and I have works." Show me your faith without your works, and I will show you my faith by my works. You believe that there is one God. You do well. Even the demons believe—and tremble! But do you want to know, O foolish man, that faith without works is dead? Was not Abraham our father justified by works when he offered Isaac—his son—on the altar? Do you see that faith was working together with his works and by works faith was made perfect?

And the scripture was fulfilled, which says, "Abraham believed God, and it was accounted to him for righteousness. And he was called the friend of God. You see then that a man is justified by works, and not by faith only."

Likewise was not Rahab, the harlot also justified by works when she received the messengers and sent them out another way? "As the body without the spirit is dead; so faith without works is dead also" (James 2: 14-26, KJV).

The text says words are justified by actions. Once again, fathers, if you love your children, don't gamble with their destiny. Get back involved with their lives and do it today. There is no time to waste; they need you. Their lives are at stake and the responsibility is yours. It is a life and death situation.

Chapter III
Biblically Speaking! Get Back To The Basics of The Bible! Father's Basic Roles! Provider

"But, if anyone does not provide for his own and especially those of his household; he has denied the faith and is worse than an unbeliever" (I Tim. 5: 8).

Basically, the father has no greater responsibility than to provide for the necessities of his family. Besides obeying the Father in heaven, there is no obligation more important for a father. But if fathers lose sight of their basic obligation to the family, then all of their other efforts are for naught.

First and foremost, fathers must always provide for the families. As seen in the text above, God has no patience for inept and lazy fathers who refuse to provide for their immediate households. The only obligation more important than reading the Word is living the Word. If the Word is read without application, that time and knowledge is wasted.

Second, another key responsibility of fathers is that of disciplinarian. It is clear from Scripture that primarily, this is the father's role. This one and some other impending facts that will be discussed later greatly increase the necessity of fathers to be in the lives of their children. As seen, they are mandated by God. First, notice father as disciplinarian.

Disciplinarian

"And you have forgotten the exhortation which speaks to you as to sons: "My son; do not despise the chastening of the Lord, nor be discouraged when you are rebuked by Him; for whom the Lord loves He chastens, and scourges every son whom He receives." If you endure chastening, God deals with you as with sons; for what son is there whom a father does not chasten? But if you are without chastening, of which all have become partakers, then you are illegitimate and not sons" (Hebrews 12: 5-8).

An amazing revelation of Scripture denotes that many characteristics of the human father are similar to those of the heavenly Father. Genesis 1:26 informs man of the creative process. Man was created in the image and likeness of God. The author of Hebrews reveals discipline to be one of God's attributes. The Bible says, "Those He loves, He rebukes and chastens."

In like manner, it applies to man. If children are not rebuked, they are not considered legitimate sons of God. The reason being, it is through discipline that both God and man demonstrate love for the human family.

Therefore, correction or admonition is not considered unjust. Correction is often the catalyst to change. A person without admonition is a person without change. There is no ambiguity in Scripture; it is clear, God's will for all of mankind is salvation (Ezek. 18: 23, 1Tim. 2: 4).

Notice II Peter 3:9, "The Lord is not slack concerning his promise, as some men count slackness; but is longsuffering to us-ward, not willing that any should perish, but that all should come to repentance." It is written, salvation is given to those who obey (Heb. 5:9). Obedience is not the means of salvation but is the responsibility of a believer (Rom. 7:1, Acts 5:32).

As God's correction is advantageous for his children, a father's correction is beneficial to his children. The Book of Proverbs, Solomon mentions the benefits of a father's admonition.

"Solomon compares the discipline of God to the discipline of a father" (Prov. 3: 12). For whom God loves He corrects, just as a father, the son in whom he delights."

The Wisdom of Solomon says, as the Lord corrects those whom he loves, a father does the same. If parents desire their children to be well-behaved sons and daughters of the highest God, correction is crucial. Those that receive little or no admonition are the same ones that more often than not leave the path of righteousness.

The desire to see the children succeed morally, physically, and spiritually must be the goal of every parent. Again, correction or admonition should not be viewed negatively. There is more hope of success for a child that received correction than one that is spoiled rotten.

Socially and secularly, correction has become increasingly taboo today but not in God's arena. In Proverbs 23:13-14, Solomon wrote, "Do not withhold correction from a child, for if you beat him with a rod, he will not die. You shall beat him with a rod, and deliver his soul from [the grave]."

God's Word specifically states that a parent is not to withhold correction from their children. In fact, it says, "A parent using the rod of correction would save the child from the grave." The word for *beat* in the above passage is derived from the Hebrew *nakah*, which is a primitive root meaning to strike.

As with all things within the Word of God, there is balance, even in discipline. However, let it not be misconstrued, this passage does not justify physical abuse that harms children. Nothing good ever comes from child abuse. Studies show that when a child is abused, later in life, he will often rebel and go the opposite way from the parents' admonition. Discretion and moderation must be the cornerstone of all actions, including admonition and discipline.

In the Bible, there is nothing more important than a parent's good example. In this passage, to spank a child is scriptural; to abuse or to cause harm, however, is not to be tolerated. As parents we need to remember that the correction of our children is a reflection of how God deals with us. While God shows correction or admonition, he never shows abuse.

Spiritual Guide and Teacher

In Proverbs 22:6, Solomon offered up a nugget of truth that if followed will benefit a child for the rest of his or her life. "Train up a child in the way he should go, and when he is old he will not depart from it." This is accomplished by both correction and admonition, along with the parent's willingness to spend time with the children. It can't be overstated that in this life nothing is more important and rewarding than family, particularly one that's doing well!

There are too many fathers who do not realize their impact on their families. They need to spend more time—quality time—with their child. It's sad to see fathers ignoring and abandoning their fatherly role. There is no time greater time spent, than in God's Word, studying, with a son or daughter.

There are some great reasons for the commands of God to teach our children about Him. He said, "You shall love the Lord they God with all your heart, soul, mind and strength. And these words which I command you today shall be in your heart. You shall teach them diligently to your children, and shall talk of them when you sit in your house, when you walk by the way, when you lie down, and when you rise up" (Deuteronomy 6:5-7 KJV).

Really before any serious training can be done to our children, fathers must have God's words in their hearts. Children will only be fooled for a little while, sooner or later and sooner than later, they will figure the parent out, particularly if he/she is not practicing what they are preaching. Hypocritical parents are dangerous to the growth and development of the child, church and themselves.

Deuteronomy six commands the parent to teach diligently, these words to the children. The word diligently comes from the Hebrew word *shanan*, which is a primitive root meaning, "to point; intensively, to pierce; figuratively, to inculcate" (New Strong's Exhaustive Concordance). To accomplish this goal, parents must teach the child God's Word when they sit in their house, walk by the way, lie down and rise up. In other words, they were to teach the children God's Word every day and live it themselves.

The Nurturing Father

Along with the duty of being chief provider, disciplinarian and instructor for the family, the father shares the task of nurturing. Usually nurturer is thought to be the role of the mother, yet highlighted throughout the book, the father plays a significant role as well. In so doing, he must be cautious not to be too soft and still be an encourager.

Paul said, "And you, fathers, do not provoke your children to wrath, but bring them up in the training and admonition of the Lord" (Ephesians 6:4). Paul addressed punishment, considered excessive and unwarranted. It will ultimately provoke a child to harbor resentment and anger.

This sometimes happen by needless severity, manifestations of anger, and unreasonable commands. God's orders of the day are: govern them, even punish them in order that they don't lose their confidence and respect, but do it all with love.

Here the Apostle Paul hit the nail on the head. This is one of the great the dangers to which parents are most exposed in the government of their children. Their sour tempers must be kept under control. Parents should never punish children while angry beyond control.

Moderation is in discipline as well. It is a known fact that many children live in abusive homes and frequently do the opposite of what the parent attempts to in force through punishment. God never promoted the abuse of children. If correction is done too harshly, defeat of the correction may occur. It is important for fathers to remember what the purpose for the discipline is. It is to nurture, not to create enduring anger or animosity.

Along with the role of nurturer, fathers must show kindness and compassion to their children. In the word of God, there are many examples where God's love for His people is compared to the love demonstrated between a father and son. Example, the Book of Psalms: "God is merciful and gracious; slow to anger, and abounding in mercy. He will not always strive with us, nor will He keep His anger forever. He has not dealt with us according to our sins, nor punished us according to our iniquities. For as the heavens are high above the earth, So great is His mercy toward those who fear Him; As far as the east is from the west, So far has He removed our transgressions from us. As a father pities his children, so God pities those who fear Him" (Psalm 103: 8-13 NKJV).

This Psalm indicates the mercy and compassion of God, a father pities his children, God pities those who fear him. The word "pity" comes from the Hebrew word racham, which means, "to love or to have compassion." In the book of Ecclesiastes 3: 1, Solomon informed us that there is a time for everything under the heavens. "A time to be born and a time to die," etc.

There is a time for correction as there is a time for love and kindness. Many times the demonstration of love will impact a child more than correction. It is a great thing that God shows love and compassion at times rather than correction and admonition all of the time.

Finally, in I Thessalonians, Paul set an example relevant to all generations. He said, "You are witnesses, and so is God also, how devoutly and justly and blamelessly we behaved ourselves among you who believe; as you know how we exhorted, and comforted, and charged every one of you, as a father does his own children" (1 Thessalonians 2: 10-11).

In other words, Paul exhorted and comforted those in Thessalonica as a father would his own children. Following his example, a father should also encourage and comfort his children. Children require their father's approval and encouragement for a well-balanced emotional state. It is divinely ordained that a son and daughter look to their father for encouragement and guidance.

In summary, a father's role is vital to the physical and emotional needs of the family. That fact cannot be overstated. Again, fathers the statistics are overwhelming, without a father, children suffer from emotional problems. Without good emotional wellbeing, a child is almost destined for crime and immorality.

It needs reiterating today because of the times in which we live that God established the family unit with one father and one mother. It is mankind's tampering with this creation of God that has brought on the mass confusion within the family. On the other hand, those that live within God's commands and structure find peace and blessings that only God gives.

Here are some additional statistics of fatherless children. The studies done and statistics recorded are endless. Fathers, please take the time to review, so that your child doesn't end up numbered in the statistical record book of the dysfunctional!

Suicide. 63 percent of youth suicides are from fatherless homes (U.S. Department of Health and Human Services, Bureau of the Census)

Behavioral Disorders. 85 percent of all children that exhibit behavioral disorders come from fatherless homes (United States Center for Disease Control)

High School Dropouts. 71 percent of all high school dropouts come from fatherless homes (National Principals Association Report on the State of High Schools.)

Educational Attainment. Kids living in single-parent homes or in stepfamilies report lower educational expectations on the part of their parents, less parental monitoring of schoolwork, and less overall social supervision than children from intact families. (N.M. Astore and S. McLanahan, American Sociological Review, No. 56 (1991)

Juvenile Detention Rates. 70 percent of juveniles in state-operated institutions come from fatherless homes (U.S. Dept. of Justice, Special Report, Sept 1988)

Aggression. In a longitudinal study of 1,197 fourth-grade students, researchers observed "greater levels of aggression in boys from mother-only households than from boys in mother-father households." (N. Vaden-Kierman, N. Ialongo, J. Pearson, and S. Kellam, "Household Family Structure and Children's Aggressive Behavior: A Longitudinal Study of Urban Elementary School Children," Journal of Abnormal Child Psychology 23, No. 5 (1995).

Achievement. Children from low-income, two-parent families outperform students from high-income, single-parent homes. Almost twice as many high achievers come from two-parent homes as one-parent homes. (One-Parent Families and Their Children, Charles F. Kettering Foundation, 1990).

Delinquency. Only 13 percent of juvenile delinquents come from families in which the biological mother and father are married to each other. By contract, 33 percent have parents who are either divorced or separated and 44 percent have parents who were never married. (Wisconsin Dept. of Health and Social Services, April 1994).

Criminal Activity. The likelihood that a young male will engage in criminal activity doubles if he is raised without a father and triples if he lives in a neighborhood with a high concentration of single-parent families. Source: A. Anne Hill, June O'Neill, Underclass Behaviors in the United States, CUNY, Baruch College. 1993

The following is a list of infamous fatherless people: Billy the kid: Sirhan Sirhan: Robert Graysmith (Zodiac Serial killer): Jack the ripper: John Wilkes Booth: Charles Manson (Cult leader and murderer): Saddam Hussein: Adolph Hitler: Mark Lepine (Mass murderer of 14): Lee Harvey Oswald: Jefrey Dahmer: "Monster" Cody (L. A. Crips GangLord).

Infamous Fatherless People:

- Billy the Kid
- Sirhan Sirhan
- Robert Graysmith (Zodiac Serial Killer)
- Jack the Ripper
- John Wilkes Booth
- Charles Manson (Cult Leader0
- Saddam Hussein
- Adolph Hitler
- Marc Lepine
- Lee Harvey Oswald
- Jeffery Dahmer
- "Monster" Cody (L.A. Crips Ganglord)

Remember, the first few chapters of the book dealt primarily with information. The next several chapters deal with inspiration. If you don't read and meditate on them, you will miss one of the greatest treats of your life. After you have read it, I know you will be inspired to give a copy to all of the fathers (and men in general) in your life.

CHAPTER IV
What Might Have Been! (Had Daddy Been There, Only God Knows?)

It all began in 1940, when a handsome young man born in Greenwood, S.C., came visiting Greenville, S.C., and met a beautiful young woman and instantly, they fell in love. The young man's name was Luther Lomax II; the young woman's name was Ola Mae Henderson.

Not long after, despite the opposition of the young lady's parents and the hard rain on that cold winter day in December (the tradition being, marriages that take place on rainy days are doomed and have many rainy days of trouble), they were married.

Obviously, the marriage did not start off with a blaze of happiness because of the information cited above. Apparently at some point soon after, the situation corrected itself because the children started to come. One after another, for twelve consecutive years, until there were nine children born to this union, six boys and three girls. Obviously, Mother did her best trying to accommodate his wishes.

What a blessing God gave them, father in particular, six strong and healthy boys, a complete basketball team with one to spare. Moreover, God's blessings did not stop there. He blessed them not only with a basketball team, but with the cheerleaders as well. They had three beautiful daughters. The blessings of God just continued, even to the point of Father receiving a namesake, Luther Lomax, III. What a God and what blessings!

Unfortunately, even with all of the blessings, Father did not commit himself to the marriage. This fact might help explain the opposition of the mother's parents to the marriage. Apparently, they detected some flaws or had some issue with Father's character. Despite Mother's blindness or weakness to the truth, the parents acknowledged the flaws and advised her of them.

However, both ignoring and disregarding their warnings and disapproval, she married the young man. It may not be true in all cases, but certainly in this one; the daughter's ignorance or ig-no-rance (refusal to listen) to her parents advice, proved to be a lifelong disaster. There are some mistakes that are recoverable and others that are not. Marriage to the wrong person is one that is hard to recover from. Remember, "Haste makes waste."

A quick word to the young of the world:

Give the parent the benefit of doubt, for it is very unusual for a parent not to want the best for their children. Although at times, parents are known to go far beyond the call of duty and become too involved in their children's lives. Sometimes they have been known to be overbearing and over protective.

Often they forget or refused to remember God's commands concerning marriage. "And Adam said; this is now bone of my bones, and flesh of my flesh: she shall be called Woman, because she was taken out of Man. Therefore shall a man leave his father and his mother, and shall cleave unto his wife: and they shall be one flesh" (Genesis 2: 23-24, KJV). Surely, it would be more politically correct, if parents were to remember all of the above.

On the other hand, there are some things that children need to acknowledge as well. They need to acknowledge that one day they will be parents also and the Bible declares, "Whatsoever a man soweth that shall he also reap" (Gal. 6: 7, KJV).

They need to acknowledge, what goes around comes around. History notes an amazing fact, the older one gets, the more he/she realizes the intelligence of their parents. That many of the things they said and did were brilliant and not outdated or old fashioned. Maybe it is true that wisdom is like wine, the older it gets, the better it is. So they say because I don't know, I do not drink alcoholic beverages. I follow Paul's advice, "Be sober and vigilant, etc. (I Peter 5: 8, KJV).

In any case, wise children listen to their parents and consider their advice. Solomon said, "A wise son hears his father and an evil son who does not receive reproof will perish" (Proverb 13: 1 Aramaic English Bible). Even if and when, the child disagrees with their parent, it is still wise to investigate the parent's suggestions. It may surprise you to discover, parents are right more often than not.

Finally, the children must understand their parents love them and would never intentionally mislead them into failure or destruction. In the final analysis, sometimes the parent's conclusions turned out to be erroneous and the child ended up being right. But still, keep in mind, the parent's suggestion was made out of love and concern which should count for something.

Case in point, despite the objection of my mother's parents, she married Dad. As they predicted, he was not the man of her dreams, but the monster of her nightmares. After the birth of each child, he disappeared for months at a time. Repeatedly, reappearing just in time to fertilize another egg and keep Mother bare foot and pregnant. After each occurrence of impregnation, he was off and running again. This went on for twelve long years.

It is sad to say but nonetheless true. The Temptation's song, "Papa Was a Rolling Stone," perfectly described my father. The song says, "It was the third of September." The date in my story was July, 1960. "That day I'll always remember, yes I will, 'Cause that was the day that my daddy died. I never got a chance to see him. Never heard nothing but bad things about him. Mama, I'm depending on you, tell me the truth."

The song says, "Mama just hung her head and said, Son, Papa was a rolling stone."

From all reports, Luther Lomax, II was a rolling stone. Where ever he lay his hat was his home. He spent the night at other's homes more than at his. He partied and drank alcohol. He chased women and most of the people in town and the community knew all about it. It was embarrassing to mother and the family. The thing that's most difficult to comprehend is how and why Mother and other mothers accept this kind of behavior from men. From the inside, out, Mother was a beautiful woman and person with a great future. She had no known insecurity issues. She was raised by a father and a mother. Although Grandmother kept Grandfather in check, sometimes a role-change such as this confuses children. All I'm saying is Mother had much more going for her than Dad.

By all accounts of the people that knew them, Mother should not have suffered such ill and inhumane treatment from such a personality. The word on the streets was he was her first love. It is said, love makes people do some strange and even self-destructive things. The old saying is, "Love makes strange bedfellows," and in this case, it was certainly true.

Thankfully for Mother, the days of her physical and mental abuse were short lived. Not long after the marriage, the husband's drinking of alcohol and the like became more serious and problematic. Also his violent nature came to the forefront.

Another word to the wise!

If the truth be told, my father had a drinking problem long before he met Mother. He also had a violent temper. Young people need to know that these issues just don't disappear after the wedding ceremony. The statistics of history, personal experience and thirty-five years of pastoral counseling testify to that point. If a person is a heavy drinker, drug attic, womanizer, manizer or has violent tenancies when met, the percentage is very high that their habits will follow them home and enter the household after the marriage ceremony.

To avoid the conflicts of impending doom, here are some serious suggestions: At the first sighting of these tenancies in the person being dated, the sensible young person needs to stop in their tracks, right then and there and think about the situation.

Instantaneously, they need to decide whether or not this is the kind of lifestyle they want to live for the rest of their lives, and are these the kind of people they want to live it with. The young person with good sense needs to accept the fact; the percentages are extremely high that they will not be able to change their partner after the marriage as so often is assumed. If you don't like them, don't marry them.

In my father's situation (As Judge Greg Mathis says), "It was more likely than not" that his drinking habits and violent nature revealed itself long before he met and married Mother. Apparently, the signs of trouble were either ignored or disregarded; possibly even both. The Bible says, "And above all things have fervent love among yourselves: for love shall cover a multitude of sins" (I Peter 4: 8 KJV). Indeed, love covers much and should cover much. But love should not cover bloody noses, or physical and mental abuse. It is not that much love in the world.

In 1955, three years after the birth of their last child, Stephen Samuel Lomax, the situation quickly worsened. In fact, it just got slam out of hand (as the old folk used to say), the violence erupted more vicious than ever before.

One night in a drunken stupor, father hit Mother in the face with his fist, broke her nose, and she bled profusely. At which time, Mother's mother (Ma-Mom as she was affectionately called by the grandchildren) got a shotgun and ran him off.

Although she did the right thing by coming to her daughter's rescue, for no parent should stand by and know that their children are being abused and do nothing, on the other hand, resorting to personal violence was not the right thing to do. The police should be called and the person or persons prosecuted as the law requires. Handling violence and criminal activity is their job and what they get paid to do. Under attack mentally and physically, do everyone a favor and call 911 and get help.

Grandmother should have called the police. However, everyone in the neighborhood knew Grandmother Henderson had a mean temperament, and "Did not take no mess." She took matters into her own hands. Unfortunately for the Lomax family, Grandmother played right into Father's hands. Apparently, he was looking for an excuse to rid himself of the responsibilities of a wife and nine children. Although Grandmother meant well, she gave him the excuse he was looking for.

Soon after the running him off with a shotgun episode, he left for good. Later, the family heard that he moved to Miami Florida, but never found out for sure where his destination was. Even today, some fifty years later, I still do not know the location. But I will say this: his departure changed the lives of his family in a negative way. Therefore, it imperative for men to man up!

Men, man up!

It needs noting that fathers should never desert their children—not even when there is a dispute with the mother or any other entity. Particularly when the dispute is outside of the household (grandmother, grandfather, sister, etc). The children are innocent bystanders and play no role in the disputed matter and should never suffer consequences for the actions of others. The children make no choice or have no say so as to who their father and mother are.

Those choices are made by the father and mother. Yet the parents need to know that they will be held accountable for their choice in this life and in the next one to come. The Word says, "Fathers never forsake your children, love them and bring them up in the fear and admonition of the Lord."

When my father left us and moved to wherever, I was the youngest and most vulnerable. I missed him greatly. I did not understand why he was not coming home any more. Why he stopped playing with me, holding and assuring me that everything was going to be all right. As a little child, I needed that assurance, love and security in my life.

After a while I was bitter, even angry that I did not have my father in my life. For many years spiritually and mentally, I was scarred beyond recognition. I did not look or feel like the human being I was created to become.

After the events of 1955, I did not see my father's face again; at least not alive. In the summer of 1960, the family was informed of his death. I will never forget that week of events. As the words of memorial to Dr. Martin Luther King Jr. are etched in stone in Washington, D.C., so are the events of that week etched in my memory bank.

At the funeral of my father there were so many people overheard saying, "what a great daddy Luther was; see how much his children loved him." That conclusion was reached because of the groaning and moaning of the children.

Fathers, please pay close attention!

What the people did not know; the groaning and moaning of the children were not out of love for Father. It was done because of the actions of Mother. She forced the children with threats of violence and a beat down like never seen before if we did not attend the funeral. In fact; I remember mother acting on her threat with my oldest sister to get her there.

I don't mean to be repetitive, but it needs highlighting to fathers across the nation, the children were not crying out of love for him, but disdain for having been forced to attend his funeral. Additionally, the sight of Mother crying caused a few more tears to flow. It hurt to see mother shedding tears, even under these circumstances.

After all of the negativity done by Father to her, Mother still shed tears for him. (There aren't too many young women today that would cry, especially, after considering the nastiness and negativity perpetuated by their ex's.) Father's desertion did a number on Mother and the children. Despite it all, someway and somehow, mother still loved him.

Reader, believe me, I feel your pain and anger. How sad to cry for such a personality, but mother was like that. She was so forgiving and loving, despite the cruel and inhumane treatment she received. Solomon speaks of women with natures like hers. He said, "Whosoever findeth a wife, fineth a good thing and obtaineth favor of the Lord" (Proverbs 18: 22, KJV).

Note the implied meaning of the verse. Although not directly stated, but strongly suggested, a man who finds a wife findeth a good thing, but if he abuses her, he will not find favor from the Lord. In Father's case, the unspoken implications of the verse were certainly accurate.

After deserting the family and the inhumane treatment of Mother in 1955, his life came to an abrupt and tragic end. In 1960, just five years after his departure, he died from Cirrhosis of the liver. What a disaster for so many lives. Because he wasn't there, what might have been for his children never was. Briefly, consider what might have been for his children.

What might have been for Luther Lomax III, his first-born son?

If Daddy had been the father who God created and ordained him to be, only God knows what might have been for the Lomax family. The oldest son, Luther Lomax III, nick named Superman, though dull in some areas and super sharp in others), possibly would have lived a long and prosperous life. Instead, he died tragically at an early age. Also nicked named Buddy (Superman), Lomax began drinking alcohol in his teenage years. He did not graduate from high school. In fact, he did not attend high school, but dropped out of elementary school.

The absence of discipline by Father was more than costly; it was fatal. Mother could not adequately perform the task of oversight because she was busy, every day, working long and hard hours, practically, twenty-four/seven just to make ends meet. Subsequently, Buddy (a name given by the community because of his easy attainable friendship) became a streetwalker both during the day and much of the night.

For extra money and to help make ends meet, he performed various chores for people within the neighborhood. While Buddy was deficient in some areas, he was highly efficient in others. One such area was memory, seemingly, he had total recall and without the aid of written notes, he could recite every detail of a grocery list. Apparently it was this supper natural memory that landed him the nickname, Superman.

Tragically however in the early eighties, he was critically injured while walking intoxicated on Laurens Rd. On a four-lane highway, in Superman like fashion, so I was told, he tried to cross this extremely busy roadway. As he stumbled and staggered, he was struck by an automobile driven by a young lady in high school.

A couple of days later, he died from brain damage and life was snatched brutally from him. Buddy, with his great memory for detail could have been an architect, engineer, lawyer, doctor, preacher, judge or another great contributor to humanity.

Yet tragically early in life, he lost the opportunity of greatness because of the lack of direction and discipline. A function that every child needs and deserves to be the best they can be. What might have been for Luther Lomax III never was.

The right discipline and direction from father would have made a difference in his life, and only God knows what he may have become. Understanding the information cited in the book thus far makes it perfectly clear, the instruction and discipline of the children was given by God to the parent, father first and mother next. Ephesians 6:4, Fathers, do not provoke your children to anger, but bring them up in the discipline and instruction of the Lord" (American Standard Bible).

Just for your information: to comprehend this scripture, listen to the following: Eph. 6:4 is a summary of instructions to the father, stated in both a negative and positive way. "Fathers, do not exasperate your children; instead, bring them up in the training and instruction of the Lord."

The negative part of the verse indicates that a father is not to foster negativity in his children by severity, injustice, partiality, or unreasonable exercise of authority. Harsh, unreasonable conduct toward a child will only serve to nurture evil in their heart.

The word *provoke* means "to irritate, exasperate, rub the wrong way, or incite." This occurs when there is a wrong spirit and accomplishments done by wrong methods; Such as severity, unreasonableness, sternness, harshness, cruel demands, needless restrictions, and selfish insistence upon dictatorial authority.

Provocation such as those above will produce adverse reactions, deadening children's affection, reduction of desire for holiness, feelings that they cannot possibly please their parents. A wise father or parent seeks to make obedience, desirable and attainable by love, gentleness and use punishment only as a last result. Physical punishment can be applied if absolutely necessary. While on the subject, please read the following article: "Spare the Rod, Spoil the Child"

"I wish that all fathers of households stand forth and practice their role. They will use the rod and not permit their children to go astray. Firmness is needed in your world that is filled with laxity, permissiveness, and degradation. "Your children have been misled by many who shall answer to the Father. As teachers they have failed in their role. Therefore, as parents you must succeed in yours."–St. Joseph, March 18, 1973

The Bible says, "He who spareth the rod hateth his son: but he that loveth him correcteth him betimes" (Proverbs 13:24) and "Withhold not correction from a child: for if thou strike him with the rod, he shall not die. Thou shalt beat him with the rod, and deliver his soul from hell." (Proverbs 23:13-14)."

Another article says: "To Spank or not to Spank (Fact sheet from the Rocky Mountain Family Council):

Is spanking an effective means of discipline for kids, or does it merely teach them to be violent? Fewer topics have generated so much emotion as whether to spank or not. First, what does the law say? Is it illegal to spank your kids? The answer is no-but parents who spank must be very careful to avoid running afoul of the law.

Colorado law defines child abuse to include any case in which a child exhibits evidence of skin bruising, bleeding, failure to thrive, burns, fractures, etc. and the condition is not justifiably explained or the circumstances indicate that the condition was not accidental. For purposes of the child abuse law, parental discipline through spanking may not be justifiable if the child is bruised or otherwise injured. Thus, spanking is not illegal, but injuring a child is.

Apart from the legalities, is spanking a good idea? Does it work? According to the American Academy of Pediatrics, about 90 % of United States parents spank, and about 59 % of pediatricians in a 1992 survey said they support the practice."

According to the academy, effective discipline has three key components: first, a loving, supportive relationship between parent and child; second, use of positive reinforcement when children behave well; and third, use of punishment when children misbehave. Many parents these days are fearful of using spanking as punishment, either because of the law or because they fear it teaches violence to their kids.

Some professional organizations of physicians and psychologists have suggested that spanking is detrimental and leads to family violence and child abuse. They have suggested that spanking teaches physically aggressive behavior which the child will imitate. But does the research support these assertions? According to the National Institute for Healthcare Research, more than 80 % of the professional publications attacking spanking were reviews and commentaries, rather than quantitative research.

When analyzing the small portion of quantitative studies that included spanking, more than 90 percent of these studies lumped together mild forms of spanking with severe forms of physical abuse without discussing why they did so. Thus, the professional organizations which advocated outlawing spanking evidently made their decisions without the benefit of the facts. Mild spanking and severe child abuse are not the same thing.

While spanking is not illegal, bruising or otherwise injuring a child is. Over the years as pastor, I have appeared with many parents or caregivers to testify on their behalf because of arrests for bruising their children or as the courts declared it to be child abuse. It needs noting that there are serious consequences for these actions. So spank, if necessary, but don't overdo it. Spanking is a corrective measure, but, is it a good idea? Spanking works best when coupled with other disciplinary measures, such as "time out." Research regarding behavior modification of children ages 2 to 6 found that spanking a child two times on either the rear or thigh helped improve compliance with "time out" for misbehavior.

These children were more likely to remain in their room after acting up if a potential spank followed if they left before the time was up. Furthermore, pairing reasoning with a spanking in the toddler years delayed misbehavior longer than did either reasoning or spanking alone.

Reasoning linked with a spank was also more effective compared with other discipline methods. Talking with the child about what behavior is expected and why-with the potential of a follow-up spank-worked best.

According to Physician magazine, "spanking should be used selectively for clear, deliberate misbehavior, especially a child's persistent defiance of a parent. It should be used only when the child receives at least as much praise for good behavior as correction for problem behavior. Verbal correction, time out and logical consequences should be used initially, followed by spanking when noncompliance persists."

According to the article, only a parent should administer a spanking, not another person. (As a father, theologian and pastor; here's my respond to the article. A reasonable and loving adult should be able to spank children. It worked for the people in pass generations and according to a great number of experts, the people back then were more honorable and respectful than today.)

Though spanking should never be administered on impulse or when a parent is out of control. Parents sometimes need a time out too. Spanking is inappropriate before 15 months of age, it should be less necessary after 6 years, and rarely, if ever, used after 10 years of age. Spanking should always be administered in private. Appropriate spanking only leaves temporary redness of skin, and never bruises or injuries. Spanking works, but must be used thoughtfully and carefully in conjunction with other disciplinary measures.

As a father, in the Judgment of God, I don't want to face the question of why I denied my children their God given rights and blessings of fatherhood. Fathers, do you?

What might have been for Mr. Robert Lee Lomax?

The second oldest son, Robert Lee Lomax, did not reach his full potential. Knowing him as I do, there was much he could have attained. Only God knows for sure what might have been, had he received the entitled benefits of his father's presence, discipline and direction.

After Father left the family, the largest responsibility of survival for the family out of the nine children fell on the shoulders of Robert. As stated above, Buddy the oldest child had some deficiencies, so Robert picked up the slack.

At an early age, he was forced to go out and find work to assist the family in their struggle for survival. He found employment, but unfortunately for his effort, he paid a price far more costly than the rest of us.

Although, because of the predicament of the family, he had no choice but to go out and do what he could. There were ten children to feed, clothe and house, and mother's income alone was not nearly sufficient to make ends meet. So, Robert was forced to assist her in the family's survival.

One day while working, trying to pump air into an automobile's tire, either, because he did not know what he was doing or not paying close attention; he over inflated the tire. It exploded in his face, leaving him severely injured. As a necessity for his survival, a metal plate was installed in his head to stabilize his brain.

Eventually, he recovered and overcame the injury, at least enough to function at a decent level of efficiency. However, the disability prevented him from becoming all he could have and should have. Still today, the necessity of outside substances helps him make it from one day to the next. The recognition for his contribution to the family is long overdue. Thanks, Brother, for the assistance.

Still, the question remains, what if he had not been denied the God given entitlements of a father's provision, protection and instruction? Only God knows for sure what might have been for him. He has a heart of kindness and generosity. As a rock mason, with the God given skills to work with his hands in the area of building and creation, he could have been a great rock sculptor, architect or artist.

What might have been for Ms. Thelma Esther Lomax?

At an early age, Thelma dropped out of elementary school. At the time, my oldest sister, Dot, had a couple of children living within our home. Thelma loved both Dot and the children greatly. In fact, when they left and went to Philadelphia to live, she was devastated.

So much so that she not only refused to return to school, soon after, she refused to leave the house altogether. With mother, seemingly working everyday from dawn to dusk in order to make ends meet for the family, she did not have time for the necessary oversight of the children's everyday routines of life.

I don't recall exactly, the length of time that went by before Mother realized Thelma was not attending school and sheltering herself away inside of the house, but eventually she did realize it. However, either because too much time had elapsed or Thelma's refusal to follow Mother's instructions to change her behavior, the situation was never corrected while Mother was alive.

After mother passed, years later due to some other changes in circumstance, she came face to face with the public again. Although limited, at least an effort was made both by her and other concerned members of the family to get her back on the right track of life.

However, without the proper correction, motivation or inspirational influence needed, Thelma went for years and years sheltered away inside of the home. Obviously, this was not a healthy situation. Thelma soon developed a serious case of "Agoraphobia;" "An anxiety disorder that causes people to suffer anxiety when placed in situations with people from which it might be difficult to escape. Webster's Dictionary states, it to be an abnormal fear of being open spaces"

As a result of Thelma's disorder not being corrected and allowed to fester, many unfortunate occurrences followed. After the death of Mother, she went through a tough time. At one point, she did not know whether she wanted to live or die. But thank God; He brought her through it.

Due to the development of Agoraphobia, Thelma missed out on so much. She missed out on romance, marriage, children, education, a job with income and even ownership of the smaller things of life. She never drove an automobile or even rode a bicycle. She missed out on friendships (outside of the family), and other simplicities of life. She missed out on as much as a regular childhood of playful games and laughter.

In fact, regrettably, Thelma missed out on the living of life. Ultimately and tragically, she died at an early age of fifty-five. With her beauty, intelligence and boldness, her future should have been and would have been bright, if the opportunities common to men and women had not been snatched from her reach.

Due to no fault of her own, she found herself in very unfortunate waters. Along with every other young person walking the dusty roads of life, she had her share of problems. Only her problems were compounded by the lack of parental attention, discipline and direction: Thus greatly limiting her possibilities of a normal happy and fulfilled life. How sick and sad.

What might have been for her, only God knows for sure. The speculations looked promising. Only if Daddy had come home and Mother been able to oversee the conditions of the household more attentively, my sister could have been anything and everything she wanted, including the nurse she dreamed and talked about from time to time. Daddies are you getting it? Your children not only want and deserve your presence, they must have it in order to be the productive persons God created and entitled them to be.

What might have been for Mr. Stephen Samuel Lomax?

Born, April 29th, 1952, the youngest of the nine children, listed here are some of his experiences and observations. Most of what I experienced (lack of disciple, direction and personal attention) were the same as those of the other siblings living within the confines of the family. The results were similar as well. There were many unfortunate and difficult moments.

Similarly, like my brothers and sisters, many of my discomforts came early in life. In fact, one of my most life changing experiences occurred in the first grade. It was there that I missed seventy-two days of the required attendance for the elementary school calendar year. Obviously, I failed the first grade, which set me on a lifelong course for failure and frustration.

During this time, life was not easy for me or any of the Lomaxes, including Mother. With Thelma, the big sister, not being required to attend school, it was a real challenge for me to continue as well. It was not easy to get up out of a warm bed every morning, step out into the cold atmosphere, bathe in cold water and dress in cold weather, then walk cold to school in the cold wind.

Everything, cold, including the children who knew I had failed the first grade, if you get my drift. Their ridicule and harassment turned a bad situation into a nightmare. As large as I was, already larger than most second graders, having to return to the first grade was humiliation at its highest level. Despite that, daily I had to gird myself up to face the obstacles of poverty: the re-washing and wearing of the same shirt, pants and socks, etc. There were many issues to overcome, but thank God for His miraculous intervention. I overcame. Thanks, particularly because at the time, I was not conscious of God.

But all praise be to Him for perseverance and knowledge; He knew what was to eventually come into my life because I surely did not. Please excuse me for pausing here to "Praise the Lord for goodness and for his wonderful works to the children of men" (Psalm 107: 8, KJV); thank you Jesus. Make note: praise is always appropriate.

Remember, Momma was not home during the morning hours to oversee my leaving the house to go to school and Daddy had deserted the family. The other brothers and sisters had their own issues, so there was very little oversight.

Feeling almost alone, I endured that nightmarish time of my life. Despite the obstacles, I returned to school and to the first grade. In fact, I not only returned to the first grade, but I completed the entire required curriculum at Allen Elementary School with honors. I was awarded the privilege to skip the seventh grade and enroll in the eighth and once again was sitting in the right educational grade of study.

Note a moment of memorable appreciation. The eighth grade holds some memorable moments for me. There were three men that helped shaped my destiny during that timeframe. Mr. Y. D. Morris was a good friend of Mother's. After the jailhouse experience for driving without a license, Mr. Y. D. Morris took the time to teach me how to drive an automobile. Having a driver's license was a tremendous blessing back then and today, still is. Sir, thank you so much for your time and effort. It may have seemed small and insignificant at the time, but it helped shaped my destiny.

The Reverend Dr. S.C. Cureton was another man that contributed greatly to my destiny. He taught Mathematics as a profession, but taught me much more as a man of God. His dress, mannerism and success as a Black man at the time impressed me so much. At school, Dr. Cureton always dressed in a suit and tie; it was not until much later that I realized he was a pastor and preacher: Though his mannerisms reflected as much.

The issue was that my irreligious background and what I was used to seeing in my neighborhood did not automatically register religion. I did not see many role models in my neighborhood that elevated my goals for life. For that I owe Dr. S.C. Cureton an enormous debt of gratitude. His talk and walk raised my self-esteem and made me conscious of the great possibilities of life. Although deceased, I want to thank him for his presence and influence.

Dr. Willis Crosby was the third man that made an impact on my destiny during that time. Currently, he is the President of S.H.A.R.E. Inc. located in Greenville, S.C. But back in the day, he and Dr. S.C. Cureton taught at Joseph E. Beck High School. Like Dr. Cureton, Dr. Crosby taught a simple course of Social Studies, but taught me much more about society. His walk and talk, his presence of confidence and appearance of success gave me more hope in the possibilities of life.

There are many people that touch other's lives and don't have an idea that they have done so. It's great to inform them if possible. It may mean as much to them now as it did to you back then. Thank you Dr. Willis Crosby for your presence and influence and may heaven continue to smile upon you.

In the eighth grade, my educational life was fighting for survival. Through the assistance of these men, it survived. Though the question still remains, "what might have been if only Daddy had been in our lives?" All of the Lomax children had great possibilities and were mentally strong.

Tribute to Noah (Seaboat) Lomax

Note a quick word about another one of the Lomax brothers who suffered also by the absence of Dad—Noah Lomax. On the ladder of age, he was next to me. As his younger brother, I immolated him as much as possible. Noah was gifted in a variety of areas. He was full of fun. If Noah could not make you laugh, there was not any laughter in you.

As an entertainer, he was extremely gifted. In a well-known soul band called the Cooter-bugs, he played the saxophone, sang and M.C. like no other around him. His potential was unlimited, but due to some bad breaks in life—with the law, sickness and other issues—he passed away far too soon at the tender age of forty-nine. I still miss you, Brother.

With Noah's talent and natural charisma, what might have been for him? If only he had not been denied the protection, provision and guidance of a father? With the right guidance, Noah could have achieved any and everything the world has to offer. Certainly, he was destined for entertainment. Only God knows what his possibilities were. He could have even been the author of this book and highlighting the achievements of his children, Noah, Noel and Bayshane, alongside me. I can not but think, what if daddy had been there for him?

At the tender age of thirteen, I had another moment of tragic possibilities. I was arrested for driving without a driver's license. I spent one night in jail. Like many of my community associates, that incident could have been a great tragedy and set me on the path to a life of criminality. Yet miraculously (notice that word again), that one night spent in jail turned out to be a lesson of blessedness.

Although another nightmarish experience, this one turned out to be a life-changing blessing. In the confines of that jail, I vowed to God that a return to jail would never again happen in my life. Never, ever will I return to jail! For more than thirty-five years or so, I kept my vow. I did not return to the jailhouse until I became a pastor and member of both the Greenville

County Detention Center Review Board and the South Carolina Juvenile Probation and Parole Board. I returned to the bars of the jailhouse only because all three institutions required visitation of the incarcerated. To God be the glory for his wonderful works to the children of men.

Once again, in the eleventh grade I stood at the crossroads of choice. A heavy decision weighed upon my shoulders. I had great potential as an athlete, particularly a runner. I ran for Wade Hampton high school and was on my way to a wonderful track and field career.

However (and there always seems to be a however in the lives of humanity, which in itself is not too bad as long as we learn from the experience), I didn't have anyone significant in my life, pushing from behind and actively motivating me. At the first obstacle, I quit the track and field activity. It was a mistake of gigantic proportions.

In fact, quitting anything worthwhile is usually a humongous mistake. So much so that it is said, *quitters never win and winners never quit*. Here is a list of a few successful children that although did not have their father's presence did not quit. In an article of ILOVEINDIA.COM, the following information was cited.

Never quit!

- "Alexander Haig, Jr.–Former White House Chief of Staff and Secretary of State. Born in the suburbs of Philadelphia on December 2, 1924, Alexander helped his mother to make both ends meet, ever since his father died at the time when he was ten years old. He started with delivering newspapers, worked for the post office and a refinery and as a store floorwalker.

  In 1969, he became the Brigadier general and in 1981, he became the fifty-ninth US Secretary of State. Despite all the struggles that he had to go through, Haig insists that his boyhood was quite normal.

- Ed Bradley–CBSTV News Correspondent and co-editor of "60 Minutes," Ed Bradley won an Emmy award. Born on June 22, 1941 in Philadelphia, Bradley's parents separated soon after his birth.
- Rickey Henderson–The star baseball player is known for his speed, powerful shots, high average and sharp batting eye. Ricky Henderson is reputed as the 'guy who keeps pitchers awake all night.' His childlike personality is as famed as his athletic skills and he simply loves children. He talks with young spectators, before, after or even during games and has handed out broken bats to children as souvenirs.

  Rickey was born on Christmas Day in 1958 in Chicago, Illinois. His mother Bobbie Henderson was a nurse and his father was a truck driver. Just a few months after his birth, his father abandoned the family. His mother moved to her parent's home in Pine Bluff, Arkansas with her eight children.
- Tom Cruise—One of the most famous, successful and highest paid actors of Hollywood, Tom Cruise was born as Thomas Cruise Mapother IV on July 3, 1962. When he was eleven, his parents got divorced and his mom took her four children to her hometown, Louisville, KY. There she struggled hard to gain financial stability including selling appliances and hosting electronics conventions.

In 1986, they were going through such financial crisis that the Mapothers wrote poems and read them to each other as gifts for Christmas because they couldn't afford anything else."

The following from "Without a father.com" adds to the list of famous people who grew up without a father or mother!

- Lance Armstrong never knew his birth father.
- Notorious B.I.G. was abandoned by his father when he was two.

- Kate Beckinsale lost her father when he died when she was six.
- Halle Berry was abandoned by her father when she was four.
- Mary J. Blige was abandoned by her father when she was four.
- Orlando Bloom lost his father when he died when he was four.
- Pierce Brosnan was abandoned by his father before his first birthday.
- Mariah Carey had little contact with her father after her parent's divorce when she was three.
- 50 Cent never knew his father and lost his mother when he was eight.
- Eric Clapton never knew his real father. He grew up thinking his grandparents were his parents and his mother his sister.
- Bill Clinton lost his father in a car accident three months before he was born.
- Stephen Colbert lost his father and two brothers in a plane crash when he was ten.
- Sean Combs was three when he lost his father who was murdered.
- Jodie Foster grew up without a father after her parents separated before she was born.
- Jamie Foxx was abandoned by both his parents and raised by his adopted grandparents.
- Cary Grant grew up thinking his mother had abandoned him when she really was in a mental institution.
- Adrian Grenier grew up not knowing who his father was.
- Laird Hamilton was abandoned by his father when he was an infant.
- Enrique Iglesias was raised mainly by his nanny, Elvira Olvarez.

- Samuel L. Jackson only met his father twice during his life.
- JayZ was abandoned by his father.
- Alicia Keys grew up without a father.
- Kid Cudi lost his father to cancer when he was eleven.
- Martin Lawrence rarely saw his father after his parents divorced when he was eight.
- John Lennon grew up without a father and lost his mother when he was seventeen.
- Jet Li lost his father when he was two.
- Shelby Lynne (born Shelby Lynn Moorer, October 22, 1968, (Age 43) in Quantico, Virginia): In August 1986, when Lynne was 17, her father shot and killed her mother and then himself.
- Madonna lost her mother to cancer when she was five.
- Paul McCartney lost his mother to cancer when he was fourteen.
- Sarah McLachlan was adopted and never knew her birth father.
- Eva Mendes was raised by her single mother after her parents divorced.
- Marilyn Monroe grew up without a father.
- Demi Moore was abandoned by her father before she was born.
- Eddie Murphy lost his father when he was killed when he was eight.
- Jack Nicholson never knew his real father.
- Shaquille O'Neal grew up without his birth father.
- Barack Obama met his father only once before he died in a car crash.
- Clive Owen was abandoned by his father when he was three.
- Al Pacino grew up in his grandparents' home with his mother.

- Guy Pearce lost his father in a work related accident when he was eight.
- Gabrielle Reece lost her father when she was five.
- Keanu Reeves was abandoned by his father when he was thirteen.
- Julia Roberts lost her father when she was ten.
- Alex Rodriguez was abandoned by his father when he was seven.
- Tupac Shakur grew up not knowing his birth father while his stepfather went to prison when he was two.
- Anderson Silva was raised by his aunt.
- Gene Simmons was abandoned by his father when he was three.
- David Spade was abandoned by his father.
- Jon Stewart was raised primarily by his mother.
- Barbra Streisand lost her father when she was two.
- Shania Twain was abandoned by her birth father.
- Liv Tyler didn't know who her birth father was until she was nine.
- Orson Welles lost his mother when he was eleven and his father when he was fifteen.

Quitters never win and winners never quit!

As with every other person alive, at certain stations in life, there are some things unknown. One of the things unknown to me was Quitters never win and winners never quit! I quit the track and field activities.

At the time, I had the potential of a football standout. But due to my failure to complete the track and field requirements, I was blocked by the coach from competing in football. As luck had it, the track and field coach was also the head football coach. The coach's disappointment in my decision to quit track and field negatively influenced his decision to allow me to sign up with the football program.

Thus the decision ended my football career at Wade Hampton High School. Although deeply disappointed, I had to acknowledge the negative result occurred because of an undisciplined, misguided, rash decision to quit the track and field activities by me. To which fully I bear the blame.

The nagging question of father's absence raised its ugly head again. If I had guidance and direction in my life, I'm sure I would not have been allowed to quit and give up so easily. With the speed and natural ability God gave me, only God knows what might have been if I had not quit?

The question is a fair one, and raised and examined because repeatedly in the lives of my children, the same type issues came up; yet as their guide and disciplinarian, I refused to allow them to give up and quit. They were forced to finish what they started. Today, they all lead successful lives. Was it accidental or coincidental, I think not?

Once again, the lack of discipline and direction was a negative turning point in my life. I was depressed over the coach's decision to halt my participation and as a result I made an even worse decision. I dropped out of high school intending to get a job and work for some of the material things in life. Again, if I had a father guiding and directing my life, things would have been different.

Instead of working toward college, I ended up working in a mill. I was hired on a job promised to me for life by the owner of the mill. The offer of the job for life sounded like a blessing, but how many people know, "Everything that sound good to you, is not good for you!

The problem was, I was hired for the strength of my body, and not for the strength of my mind. I was hired to lift and roll bales of cotton weighing more than 300 pounds from one end of the mill to the other: All night long, just rolling one bale of cotton after the other.

It did not take long to discover that this job was not the one in my dreams. It was not the job that I anticipated working for the rest of my life, rolling 300 pounds of cotton all nightlong in a mill. I only worked there one week and a half.

In fact, one night about 3:00 a.m. when I was working third shift (which was another nightmare in itself), it dawned on me that this was the night to end this nightmare of a job. I left for lunch and never returned.

Frustrated and lost without any direction, the next few years of my life were wasted doing nothing. This was another tragedy of gigantic proportions—years gone by that would never return. Another one of the real tragedies was that I did not know any better. Why I did not know any better, is a good question.

I was sixteen or seventeen years of age. Should a sixteen- or seventeen-year-old be in a position to make such decisions or should the major decisions be made by the parent? God said, "Train up a child in the way that he should go and when he is old, he will not depart from his training" Proverbs 22: 6 KJV): Another nugget for mothers and fathers to think about.

There were so many tragic and near misses in life that I felt like a cat with nine lives. The running with the wrong crowd was another train wreck waiting to happen. Life had become one tragedy after another. But miraculously (there's that word again), God blessed me.

Although at the time I did not know it was a blessing from God, but it was. Someone informed me about an organization on Camper Down Way called the Neighborhood Youth Core. I went there and they accepted my application to join them and that decision turned out to be one of the greatest decisions of my life.

I need to thank to Mr. Chuck Middlebrooks and Mrs. Smith of that group whose son was named Johnny Smith. There is one philosophy of life that played a major role in my success, always give honor and tribute to whom it is due. The scripture says, "Render therefore to all their dues: tribute to whom tribute is due; custom to whom custom; fear to whom fear; honour to whom honour" (Romans 13: 7 KJV).

With their assistance I received my GED and enrolled at Greenville Technical College studying Industrial Electronics. From Greenville Tech, the AT&T Company hired me as a technician, and I was off and running toward success.

Since the day of my father's desertion (Again, I said desertion), all I needed was somebody to help steer the ship. The misguided ship had potential to sail through unchartered waters with power and ease. The only thing missing was a captain to guide it: Much thanks and appreciation to the Neighborhood Youth Core for their concern and care.

Everybody needs to help somebody; you may never know what the seed you're sowing will someday produce. The scripture says, "He that oppresses the poor, reproaches his maker, but he that honoreth him hath mercy on the poor" (Proverb 14: 31).

In the words of King Solomon, "Now that all has been heard; here is the conclusion of the matter:" Once I received positive direction, my life changed. I went on to work for Southern Bell Telephone and Telegraph Company and AT&T.

I married a beautiful young lady, became a father of four and continued to matriculate in the field of education. In addition to the Industrial Electronic certificate, I earned four college degrees; A.A.; B.A.; M. Div.; and the Doctor of Ministry degree from Erskine Seminary in Due West, S. C.

Having overcome much to attain much, still in my life, there was something seriously missing. Still lingering was the devastating remnant of a father's absence. Even today, it still hovers over the happiness that should be enjoyed. The sad fact remains that in address or reference, I have never uttered the word *daddy*. Fathers, imagine that, denying your child such a simple, yet significant privilege.

Isn't that so sad, particularly, since daddy is such an everyday and common word? Yet, I and millions of other children like me have been deprived of this everyday privilege: The privilege to just come home and say hello, Daddy. The privilege to utter the words, Daddy, where are you or Daddy, Momma's looking for you.

The privilege to ask, Daddy, will you see who is at the door? Daddy what do you want for Christmas? Daddy, I need a loan to help me make it through this tough time. The fatherless children of the world were deprived of such a great privilege. Often, I can't help but think of the many occasions that I could have used his support.

What a wonderful privilege or God given right; just to say, I'm going tell Daddy about it and get his advice. Or I'm going to tell Daddy on you and have his backing. Sounds like such a simple privilege, but in reality, not to have it was so sad, disappointing, even devastating for a child.

Not to mention another common everyday occurrence, not to be able to say anything to my children about their granddaddy. I was not able to say to Africa, Kenya, Stephanie and Jerrell, let's go and see your granddaddy or your granddaddy asked about you: Seemingly small situations, but gigantic ramifications.

Only if Daddy had been in my life, what a difference he could have made for me. It still hurts to think about the unlimited possibilities that could have been achieved. What if Dad had been there?

Daddies give your children every opportunity the world has to offer. Be present and guide them into the right choices. Once they are grown, you can sit back and enjoy the rewards of your labor. At the very least, don't you owe them that?

Please don't miss the next chapter. It simply must be read by every father in the world. It is a eulogy of sorts to a father from the mouths of his children. The greater part of the news is reflected in the fact; the father is not dead but very much alive.

He is extended the privilege to hear for himself the words of honor, appreciation and thanksgiving.

Chapter V
Daddy's Home!
The Importance Of The Father's Presence! (In The Children's Own Words)

Under the unction of the Holy Spirit, I was led to write this book. At which time the emphasis and mission was only geared toward helping the families of the world. As I observed the world and saw so much turmoil and disarray, particular within the family structure, I was deeply saddened, disappointed, even disturbed.

The experiences of three years of service to the Greenville, S.C. Detention Center Review Board, six years to the South Carolina Juvenile Probation and Parole Board and thirty three years of pastoral duties, enlightened me of the great suffering of the family unit. At that time, the percentages of adults and children in incarceration were great and increasing steadfastly each and every day.

The reality of this dire situation came about as a result of the young people's anger, misguidance and the belief that nobody cared about their plight. Criminal behavior was a backlash to their personal anguish and pain. Persons, young and old from broken homes in every county of the state of South Carolina and the nation were incarcerated with little or no hope of a decent future.

The cause was evident; there were overwhelming numbers of people (some of my friends and acquaintances included) destroying their families through separation and divorce. Leaving the children devastated and in such disarray and dysfunction that God inspired me to both say and do something about their plight.

Each occasion when a couple of people close to me announced separation or divorce; on the inside, my spirit screamed and heart shouted, stop the madness; think about God, the marriage and the children. Can't you discern the devil's handiwork? Aren't you too wise to allow this to happen to your family? "Come on, man."

Remember the words of Jesus, "Behold, I send you forth as sheep in the middle of wolves: be you therefore "wise" as serpents, and harmless as doves" (Matt. 10: 16 AKJV). In II Corinthians 2:11, Paul warns, "Lest satan should get an advantage of us: for we are not ignorant of his (devil) devices. Don't allow the devil to get the advantage on you. Or in the vernacular of the young folk, "Don't let the devil play you."

It must be admitted, the reactions I had were so negative to their announcements and the advice given so stern and contrary to their stances, I was prepared for rejection, ridicule and serious criticisms. The stances taken on some of the issues in the book were so conflicting with society's position; I knew they would not be well received. I was not naïve in the writing. I fully expected serious rebuff, severe consequences and negative reactions. Face the facts people don't like correction.

However to my amazement and delight, the expectations anticipated did not arrive. Once again the Word of God was substantiated. "God does work in mysterious ways, his wonders to perform." When trusted and obeyed, He blesses in ways, un-thought of, and even unimaginable.

I obeyed God and expressed his word and received a great unexpected blessing. It came my way from God and is demonstrated in the upcoming chapter of the book. As stated, previous to writing the book, I had no idea that I would be so blessed personally by writing it.

Because of the climate of society, the book was written to inspire husbands and wives to consider their commitment to their family and especially their children. This consideration is a necessity if the social structure of society is to survive.

However, reading the words expressed to me by my children in the book reinforced God's foundation of society's structure; that raising your children right is tremendously rewarding and divinely necessary.

Often pastors and preachers hear eulogies about the deceased. In most cases, the deceased person never heard the words expressed being laid out so emotionally beautiful at the funeral. Many times, sitting in the rear of funeral parlors preparing to preach eulogies, I have wondered an innumerable amount of times, how sad for both the deceased and the living family member that those words were not shared with each other before now.

The deceased missed out on a blessing, and the people speaking did as well. Again, how unfortunate for both sides that the wait was so long, until it was too late to congratulate the people who played such important roles in their lives.

Truly these are great losses for all concerned. The beautiful words of thanksgiving, appreciation and congratulations should be heard by the family members while alive. "People should smell the roses while alive." It could and would make such differences in people's lives.

The beautiful words of thanksgiving, appreciation and congratulations laid on me by my children in this book made a difference in my life. In fact, it paid off (no, I meant paid down) on the great debt of sacrifice suffered on their behalf. The words were great and appreciated, but were not that great to pay off all of the many, many, many debts. Please excuse me for that moment of humor.

I am so appreciative because possibly, if they had not said what they said here on the pages of this book, I would not have known that they were affected the way they were by some of the things I said and did. My appreciation is intensified because most of the things done were small and thought meaningless, I guess they were not.

Jesus used the word, "Verily," which means truly, whenever he was about to say something highly important. Listen up: verily I say unto every father, mother and child, for motivation and encouragement, this chapter must be read and meditated upon. Hopefully to set their sights and actions toward accomplishing the necessities to one day feel the emotion and pride of a fulfilled parent. I did.

Some part of the information gathered here is to motivate the reader into writing their loved ones now (not tomorrow, next week or next month) and expressing how they feel about them (in the words of the old preacher) "before it is everlasting too late."

Hopefully and prayerfully, this chapter will continue to both motivate and inspire fathers to hang in there with their families. In order that one day, they can experience the family's heart felt actions and words of love and appreciation. Categorically, let it be declared, fathers and mothers, it is something you don't want to miss. Fasten your seat belts; the ride begins with Stephanie K. Lomax Roux. In her own words addressed to her father.

> Stephanie Lomax Roux The epitome of a father!
>
> How can I put into words the impact that my father has made on my life? This is no simple task. If I was a trapeze artist, definitely, my father would be my safety net. Obviously, he was there before birth and continues to be there even in my adulthood. My dad epitomizes the word father.
>
> A parent's job is to give a child both roots and wings. The roots provide a sense of belonging, pride in where you come from and a place to call home.
>
> The roots establish your values; they are the source of your self-esteem, your religion, your ideas and thoughts, and your overall impression of how things are "supposed to be". Essentially, your roots are who you are. The wings provide your source for flight. They prepare you for the world abroad. Whether, the discussion is about your education, trade, manners, or athletic ability, your wings are what you use to leave the nest. They are what you are.

As a young girl, I am certain that I didn't fully appreciate my father. I took his presence in my life for granted. I was embarrassed when he would yell and scream and cheer for me from the stands during my basketball games. I was humiliated when he showed up an hour early to pick me up from the eighth grade prom and actually came inside and stood there in the gym, as if any boys would want to dance with me under these circumstances. Sure, he said he forgot what time the dance was over, but I still find that hard to believe.

Also, I recall a time when he stood outside on the porch on my 16th birthday to welcome the first boy that was allowed to visit me at home. This wouldn't have been so bad, if he had not been shirtless on a freezing day in November! Surely, flexing his muscles was meant to intimidate my boyfriend who was frightened enough already. Now I know, it was dad's way of protecting me.

Even during my freshman year away at college, I was mortified when he called my dorm room and made my roommate find me to tell me that he would be calling back at midnight and I had better be in my room. Yes, I don't think I fully appreciated those situations at the time. In fact, I know I did not.

Looking back though, I can't remember a time when I didn't have his support at my basketball games. Also, at the track and field competitions, I would always look out into the bleachers and see him and mom sitting there. He woke up early on Saturdays and brought me to the meets every single one of them for over ten years straight, not missing a one. He is the reason I received a track and field scholarship at a Division 1 college, Coastal Carolina in Conway, S C.

At another very crucial moment in my life at Coastal, he came through again. It happened in 2001. At the last minute I decided that I needed to take a class trip to Costa Rica. Finally, I had made up my mind to major in Spanish and to keep pace with some of my classmates; I needed to enhance my resume by travelling abroad.

The deadline had almost passed and I still needed a few thousand dollars to sign up for the trip. I called dad and informed him of my dilemma. I asked him if there was any-way that he could make this happen; he put a check in the mail, just like that. That was the trip which led to the decision to become a Spanish teacher, and ten years later, it's still one of the best decisions I made in my life. Thanks again dad.

From speeding tickets, to automobile and even boy trouble, dad was always just a phone call away. It was dad's handling of the biggest situations as well the smaller ones which left me with my concept of what a man's role is in regard to his family.

If I ended up in a car accident, the first call wasn't to the police, it was to my dad. If there was a big spider behind the door, I wouldn't grab the bug spray, I would grab my dad. He left such a huge impression of what a real man is; that I am sure he's the reason why I expect so much from my husband as a father, provider, protector, etc.

Many fathers, less impressive are the reasons why their daughters expect so little from their husbands. A loving and caring father certainly makes a difference. If I hadn't grown accustomed to my father's activity in every aspect of my life, how would I know that those things are what a man is supposed to do? Why would I expect the things from my mate that I do? We are what we come from; we can only know what we've been taught. My father had no relationship with his father and I will never know what kind of impact that emptiness had on his life.

Yet, in some ways, I do know the answer to that question. I'm sure; the void left by his father more than not ignited his determination to be there for my siblings and me. In so doing, he accomplished something that seemingly is impossible for so many men. He broke the cycle and ended the generational curse. Thank God for that.

The contributions made by my father and mother and what they mean to me can never be fully expressed. But it is no exaggeration to say that every success that I have ever had, and every accomplishment or goal that I have ever met, belongs to my dad and mom as much as it belongs to me.

As I conclude, allow the privilege to humbly declare, the assessment of my economic status places me far from the rich and leaving me no claim to fame. But proudly I proclaim, I have achieved every goal that I set for myself as a young girl. I am happily married to a wonderfully successful handsome man. He is a pilot and a major in the U. S. Air Force. We are the proud parents of two beautiful and healthy girls. God has even blessed us with the finances to send them to the best private schools in the land. So, look out for the Rouxs.

Finally, because dad was there, I have achieved a fulfilling career. I am a Spanish teacher with two undergraduate degrees, a master's degree and hours towards my P.H.D, but more than that, I am one happy and fulfilled individual. It is my earnest prayer that my two daughters will be as blessed as I have been to have a father that they can always depend on, no matter what occurs in their lives.

Stephanie Katrice Lomax Roux

What a Blessing! Africa's next in her own words.

Subject: What a dad!
Africa U. Lomax Mccomb

Many people would contend that a good father is a provider. He gives shelter to his family and provides for their everyday needs. These same people might purport that a good father works hard to lavish his children with the latest gadgets, expensive toys, and name-brand shoes and clothes. But I would argue that a good father is more than a provider of shelter, gadgets and expensive, tangible objects. A good father provides tangible things, but more important, he provides intangible things.

I do not remember the cost of my shoes or the price tag on any blouse, but I do remember my dad attending all of my middle school, high school and a great majority of my college basketball games. I don't remember the cost of a single necklace or ring, but I do remember my dad attending every track meet and every piano recital.

At one specific track meet, I came in 2nd and the same girl beat me every single time. I was extremely upset after losing to her this time and my dad came onto the track, put his arm around me and said: I am so very proud of you. You continue to do your very best and I will always be very proud of you. My dads' comment made me feel invincible, as if I could take on the entire world and win.

Some men feel as if showing love or affection to their children somehow makes them inferior. My dad was not like that at all. He not only attended all of my games, but he told me consistently that he loved me, I was pretty, and I was smart. I now know that he increased my self-efficacy, my self- worth, but then I just felt good about being me, a Lomax.

I can recall an incident while riding the bus home from school one afternoon. (I was in the 7th grade.) This boy made fun of my nose, stating that I was sucking up all of the oxygen on the bus because my nose was so huge. Everyone on the bus began to laugh and it really hurt my feelings terribly. I later on that evening told my mom and dad about the incident and my dad again, reinforced that I was a beautiful young lady.

He told me that I was not only pretty on the outside, but on the inside as well. I recognize now that this five minute conversation impacted my perception of me. A man, whom I loved and considered my greatest hero—my dad- was saying that I was beautiful, smart and worthy. It may seem small to someone on the outside looking in, but it truly impacted my perception of myself. I have never forgotten that five minute conversation.

I had a professor in college that knew I was one course away from graduating. He decided, for reasons still unknown to me, that he would fail me in this course. Now I know what you are thinking: how can he fail you if you are getting the correct grades? But each of his exams were essay answer questions and very much subjective to the professors' discretion. I had no other problem in the classroom with any of my other professors.

And then I was one course away from graduating and my professor decided to fail me in a required course. But, he allowed me the opportunity to do some "extra credit reading" in order to pass his class. I was given a book on Zhuanxu, a Chinese emperor, and told I would have an oral examination every week on several chapters a week as "extra credit". Each week I would meet with this professor to discuss three chapters on Zhuanxu. Again, this was subjective too because it required an oral examination. After meeting with the professor 5 or 6 times, he failed me again.

This time, the result was different because my dad stepped in. He looked at the situation and concluded that something evil was taking place. He threatened to contact the NAACP, other friends in high places, even file a complaint against the professor and the college. Honestly, if it had not been for dad, I probably would have allowed this professor to prevent me from graduating because he was being really quite difficult.

But dad came to my rescue and said that this situation was intolerable. He met with the president of the University and he agreed with dad that something was not right about it all. He enrolled me in the same required course but another professor would teach the course. I received an "A" (can you believe that) and graduated. I graduated with honors because my dad, once again, arrived with his hero cape and both defended and rescued me.

But the best intangible quality about my dad is that he introduced me to Christ. I haven't ever heard my dad or mom curse. My mom or dad never came home drunk and for that matter, in thirty something years of living, I never saw them drink anything alcoholic. What can you repay someone that gave you a great foundation of the Scriptures? My sisters, brother and I attended Sunday school every Sunday, and I can't say that I always wanted to attend, but my parents never gave me an option. It wasn't a democracy: we were going to Sunday school and church.

How much is peace of mind worth? How much is true righteousness worth? How much is the knowledge that you will never be alone worth? The intimate knowledge of Christ brings peace of mind and righteousness, though undeserved. How can anyone come close to repaying God for his faithfulness? My dad and mom introduced me to Christ and I will never be able to repay them for the greatest gift I ever received. I realize that I have not been perfect and everyday continue to make mistakes, but my Christian foundation has been priceless.

As a financial analyst with a Fortune 500 company, my dad has been instrumental in my success. His tenacity in earning his Doctorate in Ministry from Erskine Seminary gave me tremendous insight in earning my Bachelors of history and Master's degree in Management and Leadership. I am even contemplating my doctoral studies, but I'd like to wait until my child is born. It was because of dad that I have aggressively confident in my present job.

So much so that I have been offered leadership positions in other states, but declined the high paying offers because it wasn't the right move for me and my family at the time. My dad taught me that next to God, the family must always be your top priority. My husband and I recently purchased a home, we have two new cars and some other materialistic valuables, but there is nothing more valuable than our intimate relationships with Christ. And when my children are born, I hope that I will be as great a parent to them as my dad and mom have been to me.

I love you dad!

Africa Lomax McComb: Price & Promotion Analyst. Food Lion, Industry

Kenya Jatun Lomax is next; in her own words.

A good dad is hard to find, but we found one!

Kenya J. Lomax

The largest impact my dad had on my life was not only being present at all of my games, track meets and voice recitals, it was just being there, constantly, my Rock! My dad, Reverend Dr. Stephen S. Lomax is some kind of a man. When I was a little girl, to me my dad was the strongest, tallest, smartest, most handsome man in the world. It's no wonder my siblings and I are, although very different, spoiled and sometimes over confident. To every problem, my dad's words were the same, you are "Lomaxes," and that was good enough to solve any problem.

There are so many stories of how my dad embarrassed me, fussed at me, whipped me and made me proud all at the same time. One of the most memorable occasions occurred when I was 18 years old, fresh out of high school and attending my first year of college. A new urban movie came out and the local radio station was giving out free tickets to the premiere.

My sister Stephanie and I went along with many of the other students at my school. I will never forget it. It occurred on a Thursday in December of 1995 and I was one of the lucky recipients of a couple of tickets. Yet, in order to go (because of dad's strict rules), I had to take my little sister Stephanie who was 15 at the time with me. As far as I knew, the weather forecast that day was good and fair. So off to the theatre we went. When we arrived, we just went into the theatre. At the time we went in, the weather was sunny and normal, although, it was a little chilly.

We had been in the theatre approximately an hour or so and all of a sudden I heard a voice that was very loud and familiar coming from the back opposite side of the theatre. Each time I heard it, it was louder and louder, yelling, "There's a blizzard outside, I'm looking for Kenya and Stephanie Lomax!"

Immediately, there was laughter like I'd never heard before bursting out all over the theatre. Dad was walking up and down the aisles (of course I heard him but there was no way I was answering). Some guy yelled "She's gone and I hope you will soon be leaving with her." The laughter continued, but my dad answered back and said, "I said, there's a blizzard going on outside and I'm looking for my daughters, Kenya and Stephanie Lomax. You all can stay in here, if you want to!"

By then, my little sister, Stephanie was really scared and attempted to stand up. But I jerked her back down in the seat and continued to wait for the other people to first follow my dad out of the theatre. Then the lights came on and we walked out and there dad was, standing and fussing with the theatre attendant. He was yelling at him for allowing all of these kids (who happen to be Black) to remain in the theatre while unknowingly were in the midst of one of the worst snow and ice storms I ever saw.

We walked outside and sure enough, there was a blizzard taking place. The ground was covered with snow and ice and hail was coming down by the truck loads. It was so bad that dad didn't allow me to drive the truck back home. We rode home in his car and left his other vehicle there. Although, scared and embarrassed, I was overcome with pride, security and love, all at the same time.

It's been like that all throughout my life. My dad has been there even when I didn't want him to be. In high school everyone knew who my dad was. Being one of the three "Lomax Girls" as we were known, was like being a forbidden fruit. Many guys wanted to take us out but they knew they had to make it past our dad. He was always around except during school hours which I believe if he could have, he would've sat right behind each of us in class.

We were popular PKs and normally didn't have many problems with kids. But once there was a guy who lived down the street from us. He was a senior and I was a freshman. He used to pick at me all the time but of course I never told my dad because I knew he would overreact. One particular basketball game, "this guy (who I remember, but will not name) picked me up and pushed me down and I fell over some of the bleachers.

My dad was there and just so happened, he saw the actions of the guy and became infuriated. He ran over to the guy, standing over him said something to him. To this day, I still do not know what was said. But whatever it was; scared the bully and to this day (some twenty years later), never had any more issues with him.

Dad not only came to my rescue with bullying children, but also with bullying adults. In fact, they received the worst scolding. I will never forget when I was in the 4th grade and my reading teacher, unhappy with the scores of my reading group, threw a workbook at me. Once I again I went home and told dad. At first, he had trouble believing it and went to confirm my story with a fellow classmate. Once confirmed, dad was enraged.

The next morning he took me to school. We went straight into the principal's office and dad had the teacher called to the meeting. Once again; I 'm not sure what was said, my parents were from the old school of thought and kids were not included in "grown folks business." But what I did remember was this, after the meeting, my teacher was red faced and later that day she not only apologized to me, but to everyone in my reading group. All of my classmates were envious of me and teased that if the teachers did anything to them, they would call my daddy.

Although they teased me about it, little did they know they were not insulting me, because I always knew, if any wrong was perpetrated on me (as long as I was right), I could always count on dad.

Listen up, parents and children!

Unlike many parents today, Dad made it very clear to me and my siblings that if we claimed mistreatment, he would investigate it. He also made it very clear to us that if we ever came home with false stories or made up lies and he was made to look like a fool because of it, he would have our hides.

Dad was not only our support to the outside world he would protect us from each other. I was fortunate enough to have the darkest complexion in my immediate family until Jerrell came along. Like all siblings tease each other, my sisters taunted me about it. I must admit that it was a very sensitive issue.

Again, unlike most parents today that allow sibling rivalries, my dad did not tolerate it. He chastised my sisters and me (whenever I had the upper hand on them and returned the favor). He would make us apologize, hug, kiss and tell each other, "I love you." We hated to say those words, especially in the heat of battle and argument.

Yet, the tradition of making up immediately worked and still is honored by all of the children today. Although we live hundreds of miles apart, we are extremely close and communicate almost daily. The sole reason for our closeness is attributed to our parent's obsession to not allow things to fester or build up; but settle the issue, immediately. There is a passage of scripture that sometimes dad quotes, "Be ye angry, and sin not: let not the sun go down upon your wrath" (Eph. 4: 26 KJV). This has been a blessing to our family.

There's another important ritual that our home maintained. When dad came home from work, we ate dinner at the dining room table together. He asked us questions about our day and we had to answer. There weren't any one word answers either. You had to tell about your events of the day. I am a single mother, but I still carry on this tradition with my son. I ask him about his day; yet I don't have to press him to answer, I have to press him to stop.

To dad's credit, he didn't miss any important moments in my life. He's been there throughout the good, bad and the ugly. The best moment of my life came when I birthed my son, Stephen S. Lomax, II. It seems constant and everywhere I go, people ask me why did you choose that name for your son? As far as I am concerned, there was no other name that I wanted to give my son other than the name of my dad. He was the man that I wanted him to emulate.

Although at the time I birthed my son, I was 26 years of age and thought I was grown. Still, I was disappointed in myself for having a child out of wedlock because I know dad was disappointed in me. He had made it very clear that it was not the way God intended. Yet, he was there with me for 18 hours of labor; he and mom never left my side. When my son took his first breath my dad was there and didn't say anything negative. He looked at me with pride and said, "Kenya you did good; look at him."

No matter what and how the circumstances lined up, in every key moment of my life, whether or not he agreed, he put his personal stance aside and showed me love and forgiveness. Once forgiven, dad never brought up the issue again unless we were making light of the ordeal.

Daddy's impact on my life has been huge. In fact, partially, I blame him for my single status. If he had not been such a major positive influence and such a great role model, maybe I would not be single. Maybe, I would be like so many of my female friends looking for love from any male, under any circumstance, no matter what the person have or don't have to offer.

But because dad has always told and showed us how much he loves us, I can't pretend that I don't know what true love is. I've been trained too well, to accept anything from a man. If he doesn't have anything to bring to the table and cannot provide for my son and myself, I am better off remaining single. Somebody sang, "I can do bad by myself." In some way, the man must enhance my life and my son's life.

It is sad to say, the majority of men today have no clue as to how to be a man, much less how to be a father or husband. It's hard to find a man with the standards and qualities of my dad. As a child, I always said, I never wanted a husband like my dad: too many principles, rules and regulations. But as an adult and as a Christian woman, my views have changed. The man in my life must possess some of the same qualities, if we are to have a positive future together. When dad finally walks me down the aisle, he can rest assured, he will give me away to a man that will lead and direct my family as he did.

If I would have been given the privilege to speak with Jesus personally and He would have allowed me to create a dad from nothing but dust, I would not change a thing about Stephen S. Lomax, my dad. Daddy you are my mentor, teacher, disciplinarian, pastor and above all you are my friend! Thank you for being everything to me. I love you and mom with all that is within me!! You guys Rock!!

Finally, I am what I am because of dad and mom. I graduated from high school. I attended Greenville Technical College. Currently, I attend Walden University working toward a Bachelors of Science Degree in accounting. I am the owner and CEO of Lomax Fast Taxes. A great tax company located in two locations, Greenville and Fountain Inn, S. C. "To God be the glory for the great things he has done."

Jerrell's next: A son's perspective; in his own words.

A dad like no other!

Jerrell Lanier Lomax

Having my father in my life means everything to me. My mother does as well. She was a blessing and taught me how to be a gentleman. She taught me politeness, manners, cleanliness and many other quality things. What a mother! Yet there were some things that mom didn't, nor couldn't teach me. In fact, there are some things that a mother cannot teach a son. But thank God I had father and mother in my life. My father taught me how to be a man.

Growing up, I remember how he would take me along with him when he did his odds and INS. He explained to me why, when, where and how he did the things he did. He always said, "Boy you need to learn these things because tomorrow is not promised to any of us and I am not going to be here forever."

Also I remember when I was young, everything terrified me. There was one time in particular, dad sent me to jump off one of the batteries in the car. When I went to do it, the battery sparked and I dropped the jumper cables and ran. He came out of the house and said, "Boy what is your Problem?" When I told him what happened, he immediately looked at me and said, "Stop being afraid of everything, especially things you can control." Immediately, he fixed the problem and went back to his study for more research on one of his books.

His calm, cool and collectiveness changed my entire outlook on fear and confidence in my-self heightened. Instantly, I began doing things on my own that normally I had been afraid of. Mainly, there were two reasons for my change in attitude. First, I didn't want to see that look of disappointment on his face again. And second, I knew dad was right, it was time that I learned to do these things on my own.

This lesson may sound simple, but as I look back on it today, it was huge. Now that I am on my own, I cannot afford to be fearful of the little necessary chores in life. Truly, I am blessed to have my father in my life. To be completely honest, I don't know how my life would have turned out without his love and guidance. To think of life without him is a scary and empty thought. As a child, the many things he taught me; the lessons I learned from him growing up from a teen into young adulthood definitely made the difference in the choices I made for myself.

At times, I thought he was by far too hard on me. Now that I am older I see things differently. When I thought he was being too hard on me, really, he was not being hard enough considering some of the dangerous things, I was involved with.

Parents, let me interject a point here!

I know you believe that you know all there is to know about your children. Also, I know that you think your children are different than everybody else's and yours are special. They are special, but so is everybody else's. The main point of this interjection is not to insult or antagonize you. It is to say, however, categorically that your children and mine are like everybody else's.

In fact, the children today are just like you were I were when we were children: Except more technological with the advancement of the computer, etc. Even with that, still, the simple truth is, all children are just that, children. They look different, even talk and walk different but still, deep down, they are the same.

Sometimes, when caught in between a rock and hard place, they lie. Other times, they do things behind their parents back. Not some children, all children, including yours and mine. The facts that have just been stated are very important information, I hope you take it for what it is worth and use it wisely. The facts were learned and verified by both data and experience as I sit on the Greenville, S. C. Detention Review Board and the S. C. Department of Juvenile Parole and Probation Boards for over ten years combined.

The facts are; if you allow your children to run with the wrong crowd, they will participate in activities that the crowd is engaged in. Parents need to be aware also, it is not always an easy task to distinguish who the wrong crowd is. Some of the very people, you think are great influences on your child, in reality, many are the worse.

The suggestion is, for you to always be alert, watchful and investigate. Use the agencies available to assist you in the endeavor keeping your child safe. This is not only the advice of the writer but God's advice as well. I Peter 5: 8, reminds mankind to "Be sober and vigilant, for your adversary the devil, as a roaring lion, walketh about, seeking whom he may devour."

Despite popular opinion, the devil and his demons are real. They are constantly going to and fro and up and down in the earth, looking for the old and young for destructive purposes. For more on the Devil, see the final chapter of the book, entitled, Fathers and the Biblical realities of the Devil. And Daddies and the Devil! "The solution being, Be watchful and alert.

Another fact; trust your children, but don't be foolish. When some things alarm you, be alarmed. A parent's intuition is a great tool, so use it. Additionally, if something sounds too good to be true, it is usually is. Again the suggestion is, pay attention to the activities of your children. Monitor them and their friends, all of them, including the son and daughter of the lawyer, doctor and the preacher. In the end, you will be glad you did.

The end of the interruption!

I can handle problems much better than most of the young men my age. Dad made sure I was going to succeed and helped prepare me for whatever might come my way. I can't forget the encouraging words he told me at the most crucial times in my life. He always said, Jerrell, "You can do anything you want to, if you put your mind to it. Start standing up for what you believe in and always remember who you are, you are a Lomax."

Just the other day I was having a conversation with a few coworkers. They were discussing things that they would do for money. As they were naming different things, I looked at them like they were crazy. (In reality, they were not only crazy, they were immoral.) At my look of disbelief, each one of them looked at me and said, "Jerrell, you know you would be right in the midst of it with us, if someone offered you ten million dollars!" To them I replied, no, I would not. I have too much dignity to belittle myself for money!" Of course they laughed at me, but the joke was on them.

All of us are the same age. But the fact that at an early age, my father taught me to always remember who I am and to stand up for what I believe, the difference between them and myself is huge. Their hearts, minds and values are completely opposite of mine. They will do anything for money; maybe, even sell their own souls. I am so glad that I was raised with morals. The lessons taught by dad are priceless; you can't just walk into Wal-Mart and pick them up right off of the shelf. They were instilled in me by a loving and moral father.

Also, I watched how dad interacted with my mother and sisters. He treated them so beautifully. He loved each of them and never disrespected any of them. Any man can be a "Dad" but it takes someone special to be a "Father." I say this because my father not only helped make us, he helped raise us. He is not only a great father, but a friend, mentor, protector, leader, teacher and provider. He made sure we never needed anything. We didn't get everything we wanted, but we still had more than enough of what we needed. He was always there for us.

The time of the day didn't matter, the distance or even his schedule of prior engagements, he still made time for us. He always showed up to support us. When we played sports: If he saw that we could do better than what we were doing, you would know it along with everybody else. He would holler and yell from the stands. It was embarrassing at first, but then I realized that it was his way of showing me that he believed in me. His faith in me carried me a long way in life. It was because of dad, I feel that I have accomplished much in my short twenty four years of living.

However, there are too many deeds left undone and accomplishments unfulfilled from people in society today because they didn't have anyone who believed in them. I am glad that I have a dad that both encouraged and believed in me. His position of non-foolishness pushed me into the military. Now I am a much stronger young man with a name for myself. At present, my rank in the United States Navy is E-4, and soon will be an E-5. I mentor a group of teenage boys in the city of Newport News, VA; where I share the same knowledge and wisdom that my father shared with me.

Before joining the U.S. Navy, I graduated High School and did further studies at Greenville Technical College. Currently, I am enrolled at St. Leo's University in Norfolk, VA; pursuing a Bachelors of Science Degree. Once completed, I will enroll in a Master's program at the College. Finally, I am an amateur comedian and have performed in cities across the country. The few accomplishments achieved thus far occurred as a result of the faith and belief that dad has in me.

The words of appreciation for my father could go on and on and on. He has done so much for me. But the number one thing he has done and continues to do each time we talk, (which makes me emotional every time I think about it) is, he tells me he loves me. At the end of each and every telephone call, he says, "I love you."

Every time I come home from being overseas, he always greets me at the door with a hug. That means the world to me. I acknowledge without hesitation, there is no love greater than a mother and a father's (except Christ). Especially a father's love because in today's society, the absence of the father is so common.

Finally, if more men that have kids were to see them and spend more time with them and tell them, "I love you," many of society's ills would disappear. Like so many others, I have done wrong and made mistakes in my life. There were times that I failed and wanted to give up, but I had a strong man standing behind me. My father has always been there pushing me onward.

He never passed judgment on me (although he let me know many times when I was wrong). Also, he never let me quit. He allowed my sisters and me to explore many challenges, but he always said," once you sign up and I pay the money for your enrollment, you will not quit until the end." Constantly, he reminded me that life is not always easy and there are things everybody has to go through to learn and better prepare themselves.

Dad did not allow me to have a pity party or sit in the pits of despair for too long. He always motivated me to get up and continue living. The things he said and did both helped me move forward with my life and make it to the top.

I am so thankful to my father for being my foundation. Houses built upon great foundations are strong and last for long times. Even when the storms of life blow and create minor damage, the house can be rebuilt easier because of the strong foundation. I built my life's house on the foundation laid by my father. Yes, some storms and disasters came and shook the house and caused damage, but the foundation stood and is still strong. For that, I am eternally grateful and blessed and for all of the rest, my father has done.

Jerrell Lanier Lomax

Next, Mrs. Frances Delores Shaw Lomax:

A great word from a wife and mother!

Mrs. Frances Shaw Lomax

To further the cause of children, allow me to put my spin on the chapter. I have been very blessed and fortunate in that I cannot speak of what it was like not to have a dad at home. I was born into a proud two parent loving, Christian home. My birth mother, the late Sarah Fuller Shaw passed away during the childbirth of a brother when I was two years old. My dad remarried Ms. Eunice Clark

Shaw when I was four years old and praise God, all of my parents were saved.

My dad was a born again Baptist preacher who not only talked the talk but walked the walk. My dad was a man that loved to laugh. Even though he went to be with the Lord some 27 year ago, even now, I cannot run into any of his friends or our older relatives without them sharing a funny story with me about the Shaw twins (my dad, Talmar and his identical twin brother, Almar).

Although dad was fun loving and loved to laugh, trust me, we kids knew where to draw the line. Truly, I cannot remember my father being upset with anybody other than my siblings and I (and occasionally my mom) his entire life and he was 64 years of age when he passed. That is not to say that he was never upset with anyone, it is to say, if he was I never knew it.

He and my mother were very "old school" and believed divorce was not an option and "if you spare the rod, you spoil the child." My dad was very strong in the faith and from what I'm told about my birth mother and what I saw firsthand of my step mother, they were strong as well.

My three brothers, Lindsey, Charles and David, my five sisters Sharon Barksdale, Sandra Smith, Lisa Shaw, Shelia Mobley and Rita Anderson and I dreaded the words, "Just wait 'til your daddy get home" (Well, maybe not Shelia and Rita because mom and dad had softened by the time they came along and they had it made).

As an adult I have often wondered, but still have not figured out why it is that my children respected or for the lack of a better word 'feared" their dad more than me. During the early years of our marriage, after Lomax was saved and quit the soul band, he began working full time. Plus he was going to school and pastoring a church all at the same time. So there were many early mornings and late nights that the kids and I did not get to see much of him.

Many of you ladies understand what that means. I did most of the disciplining or should I say I handled all of the small stuff and believe me, it was a lot of small stuff. But when the kids really messed up and did something that warranted his attention, to really ruin their day, all I had to say was, "Just wait 'til your daddy get home." I'm sure I handed out more whippings, at least five times as many but for some reason, his were the ones they feared.

However as I meditated upon it, it was no different with my dad. In my youth, mother (what I called her) whipped the children more than he did. But for the serious devilment violations, she would say, 'Just wait until your daddy get home."

Through my father's rearing, I already knew the importance of having a godly man in the house. I thank God that the kids were blessed to learn it early as well. God, in His infinite wisdom placed man at the head which means provider and protector. There are many times that I don't understand it but after thinking about, I'm glad He did.

Down through our history, mothers and grandmothers have been the ones to lift up and support the children; unfortunately the same cannot be said of fathers. Even though Lomax has not been perfect and I don't know any who has (that is a book, I could write), I am happy that he took seriously the mandates placed on the man by God. Solomon said, "Train up children in the way they should go and when they get old, they will not depart from it" (Proverbs 22: 6).

Also he took seriously the mandate "to provide for and protect the family." "But, if anyone does not provide for his own and especially those of his household; he has denied the faith and is worse than an unbeliever" (I Tim. 5: 8). Fathers don't be infidels.

The word of God tells us that "all things work together for the good of those that love Him and are called according to His purpose" (Roman 8: 28, KJV). It is unfortunate and sad that Lomax grew up without father's presence and protection and all that a father brings to the family table.

However, I am a grateful benefactor because it impacted him positively. So much so that he aspired with great determination to be a great dad. The children actually grew up thinking that there was nothing their dad couldn't do. It did not matter what the problem, just tell dad and he would handle it.

At the present time my only grandson, my husband's namesake; Stephen Samuel Lomax II is being reared by our daughter, Kenya, a single mother. But I am grateful that his granddaddy (Grampa), as he calls him is still alive, healthy and able to "stand in the gap" so to speak.

My grandson's (Noodle, as we refer to him) dad is a truck driver. Fortunately he is involved in his life and supports him financially and physically often. His work schedule causes him to be absent and unfortunately, there are times when Noodle does not see him daily, weekly and sometimes, not even monthly.

But thank God, Grampa is a constant presence of support in his life. He knows his teachers personally. He attends all of the special lunches at school and picks him up from school two or three times every week or every chance he gets. As an incentive for him to do well in school, Noodle knows when Grampa picks him up and if he has a good report for the day, he will be treated special and taken straight to Chic-Fil-A for ice cream and chicken nuggets.

On the other hand, if he has done poorly, part of the punishment is to listen to Grampa preach and teach an early sermon: Although it is not Sunday, the usual day for Pastor Lomax to preach. If by chance, Noodle's poor performance is the first of the week, once they arrive home from school, he is sent straight to the room with no T.V.

If it is his second or third poor performance either scholastically or behaviorally, it's straight to the room with an application of Proverbs 13: 24. (Fathers, look the passage up. You need to be familiar with it to Biblically rear your children.)

Also, Noodle knows that whatever his extra-curricular activity happens to be, whether football, basketball, Taekwondo, drums, actor in a play or whatever is postponed until his behavior improves. On the other hand, he knows that when doing well in school, he can count on mom, aunts and uncles, granny and for sure Grampa's support.

Additionally, I am grateful that my two granddaughter's father, Air Force Major, Jaron Roux knows the importance of a father's presence in a child's life. He is a pilot. When he and Stephanie, our baby daughter, the Spanish teacher met and married, his high paying job required him to be away for months at a time during the year.

This occurred before the birth of his two beautiful daughters. Having been reared without his father and the issues that followed, he knows that money is not as important as being home at bath and story-time for his daughters, Zhain and Zion. He gave up the extra work for extra money and took less paying assignments in order to gain more. I hope you got it. He gave up some things materially in order to gain some things, spiritually. He gave up extra money to spend more time with wife and family.

His reward is great. Every time he comes home and hears and sees his children express their joy and happiness to see him walk through the doors. On this subject, the list of testimonials is long and overwhelming. It is joy unspeakable to have your children express their excitement, love and appreciation just for your walking through the doors.

There is no level of greater satisfaction and fulfillment than for a father or mother coming home every day to a family that not only knows them personally, but shows them love, appreciation and admiration. Take it from one who knows, this experience is priceless. Kenya, Stephanie and Jaron are great parents and are keeping the tradition of loving families alive and well. Keep up the great work.

Our first born Africa is expecting her first child. Her husband Todd McComb is a defensive back coach at

Catawba University and doing a great job. (If there is a division I head coach reading this book, coach Mccomb will do you good. Just trying to assist the family, this is what loving families do.)

Like Africa, he had the privilege of growing up in a two-parent Christian home. I am sure they will be great parents to our unborn grandchild, as will our son, Jerrell when he finds Ms. Right and become a parent.

In conclusion, let me put on my "mother" and "mentor" hat and speak to any young married lady reading this book who's struggling with the nagging question of "shall I leave or shall I stay." During the course of my thirty-nine-year marriage, the question crossed my mind here and there. Here is the advice I give concerning the question: unless he is physically or mentally abusing you, don't be so quick to give up on your marriage and the family.

Know that your decision will negatively or positively impact more than you. It will dramatically affect the children and the grandchildren as well. Many times, your children's dysfunction is deep enough to infect their children: Thus keeping the dysfunction alive for generations.

There are too many kids struggling with emotional problems because their dads are living in another house across town, raising someone else's children. Ladies, no matter how well grounded your children appear to be, it does affect a child's emotional state to know that the kids living in the house with their dad are being blessed with his daily love, attention and presence. While they are being neglected and treated like stepchildren.

Yet if there is physical or mental abuse from anyone, no matter who the person might be, no child should suffer that. Ladies judge the situation well, there is much at stake. There are generations of your descendant's lives on the line.

Families that pray together stay together!

There is nothing more enchanting and rewarding than families coming together and preparing to celebrate the birth of Christ. Along with Easter, the Christmas season is the busiest and one of the most exciting times of the year. As in times past and gone, I look forward with great anticipation a wonderful gathering of friends and family.

After dinner, the lighting of candles and prayer in memorial of the deceased members of the family is done. Followed by the exchanging of gifts, playing games and caroling on Christmas Eve with the siblings and their families and the children; what a festival of delight.

Once the children and grandchildren have finally been put to bed at my house, after the tree has been undressed beginning at 12:01 on Christmas morning and after the traditional scavenger hunt that started with my kids over thirty five years ago which has been handed down to the grandkids, we sit around the dining room table sharing breakfast on Christmas morning.

Dad, now granddad sits at the head of the table and me (the wife and mother, now grandmother) at the other end surrounded by the children, their spouses and grandchildren. It's times like these that I am particularly grateful that Lomax and I weathered the early storms. Looking back, these storms were very similar to the weather storms. They came up quick, designed not to last long. Yet, many lasted much longer because we gave them wind, lightning and thunder and increased longevity of life.

In the final analysis, make no mistake about it, it is very important to have daddy home. Also, it isn't funny or ironic how history repeats itself. The phrases that mother used to say to me that I hated to hear, I in turn say them to my children. Phrases like, "You are getting too big for your britches, I am going to have to bring you down a button hole or two. Don't make me slap the fire out of you. You just wait until your daddy get home."

Just Wait 'Til Your Daddy Gets Home

When Noodle is spending the night (as he does every weekend unless he is at his dad's) and does something that warrants it, I now tell him, "Just wait until your granddaddy get home." To which he always say, "aw come on granny, don't tell." I guess I'm getting soft in my old age because sometimes I don't tell.

Parents, if you were touched and would someday love to be so remembered and admired by your children and family, please read the next chapter. How to attain and maintain loving families as instructed by God, the ultimate Father. You will be blessed.

CHAPTER VI
How To Attain And Maintain Loving Families! Cohabitation Is Not One Of Them Beyonce' Has A Point! The Importance Of Two Parent System! (Husband And Wife, Male And Female) Everybody's Has A Part To Play!

"And God blessed them, and God said unto them, Be fruitful, and multiply, and replenish the earth, and subdue it: and have dominion over the fish of the sea, and over the fowl of the air, and over every living thing that moveth upon the earth." (Genesis 1:28, KJV).

"Adam named his wife Eve because she would become the mother of all the living" (Genesis 3: 20, KJV).

Most people are aware that they were created with certain innate desires and urges: The thirst for food, water, sleep and generally, survival needs. There is also an innate desire within the male species to protect and provide, which is also prevalent among the lower animal kingdom. The lions, tigers, dogs chickens, birds, eagles, etc. all have demonstrated it.

But with man, it is more highlighted. It is a dominant component of both who man is and who he was created to become. It is in his biological make up and DNA. To satisfy the desire to protect and provide, God installed the institution of marriage and fatherhood. It is regrettable that more and more young men are electing not to marry and attempting to satisfy the God given longings in ways contrary to his words.

One such way is fornication. It needs stating that fornication (any form of sexual activity outside of marriage) is still sin. Though mankind and society accepts it more and more as normal human behavior, it is still unacceptable before God.

Cohabitation (Shacking) is another device of the devil designed to fool men and women into relationships that supposedly substitute marriage, but in reality separate God from mankind. It needs stating clearly and emphatically, relationships outside of marriage are not acceptable before God. The Scripture declares, "Marriage should be honored by all, and the marriage bed kept pure, for God will judge the adulterer and all the sexually immoral" (Hebrews 13: 4 NIV).

Additionally, bearing and rearing children outside of marriage is not only sin, but sinfully foolish. Every person, particularly women, need to examine the philosophy of cohabitation (shacking). This specification directed toward women occurred not by accident, but by divine providence.

Women, listen up.

God made the woman attractive to man for a reason. Her attractiveness, beauty and innate grip on man are tools of leverage and should not be given away without serious thought. To give away such an advantage is much more than unwise, it is counterproductive spiritually and harmful, physically. For women to be effective in their dealings with men, they must learn to use their tools of leverage wisely and not wastefully. They are always to be used in the confines of God's commands, which mean marriage and marriage only.

Cohabitation (shacking) is sin for both the man and the woman, but it is more foolish for the woman than for the man. In cohabitation, the man achieves his goal of satisfaction with the least amount of commitment. If and when the attraction diminishes, the man has more freedom to look for and move on to "greener pastures." The teaching of Momma to the women in my family seems appropriate here. Speaking of pastures, Momma said, "Only a fool buys a cow, when you can get the milk free." A simple statement, but loaded with wisdom.

Moreover, the cohabitation philosophy is highly unstable in the maintenance of the family unit. As stated above, without marriage, the man (and in some instances the woman) will desert the living arrangements with more ease. It is a fact that cohabiters don't possess the same commitment to the family unit as their married counter parts.

At the very least, married couples vowed to God, the preacher and host of other witnesses to remain together until death. Although, very few keep the vow. Still, they stood before God and mankind and made it while cohabiters took no such stance or made no such public commitment.

In fact, at least part of the reason for their status as cohabiters is reflected in that, they refuse such public announcements. The argument could even be made that secrecy of the relationship is one of the attractions of cohabitation and based upon the evidence, it would be a valid position.

Almost in every instance of cohabitation, at least one of the person's involved is against public awareness of their situation. There are many persons from traditional and religious homes that are embarrassed for their parents to know their cohabitant status. Yet, the issue of secrecy adds more weight to the instability of cohabitation and another main reason, participation is unwise.

In an article concerning cohabitation, entitled "The Verdict on cohabitation Verse Marriage" by Jeffry H. Larson, Ph.D., LMFT, CFLE, is a professor of Marriage and Family Therapy at Brigham Young University and author of Should We Stay Together? A Scientifically Proven Method for Evaluating Your Relationship and Improving its Chances for Long Term Success (San Francisco: Jossey-Bass, 2000), the following findings were recorded.

"Although some couples say they cohabit for convenience (e.g., only one apartment to clean) or to lower their cost of living (one apartment is cheaper than two), most adults say they cohabit for one or more of the following reasons: (1) for emotional and sexual intimacy without the obligations of marriage; (2) to test their compatibility; (3) to prepare for marriage by practicing living with someone "24/7"; and (4) to better know each other's habits, character, and fidelity."

Some people perceive cohabitation as a way to have a more intimate relationship without the risks of divorce or being trapped in an unhappy marriage. On the other hand, others believe cohabitation is the first step to marriage. Hear me good, the statistics are overwhelming that cohabitation does not lead to marriage in the majority of cases. Additionally, among the few cohabiters who do marry, their chances of divorce are actually increased. No one has ever found that cohabitation makes a positive contribution to marital stability.

An article in the NY Times on 4/14/12 supports my opinion that living together before marriage is not a good idea. Here are four of seven Reasons Why Cohabitation Increases the Chance of Divorce and should not occur!

First, people willing to live together are more unconventional than others and tend to be less committed to marriage as an institution. These two factors make it easier for them to exit a marriage later if it becomes unsatisfying. Marriage after all, is a unique relationship that assumes a vow of permanence.

Most cohabiters fear, or are not ready for such a permanent relationship. For them, according to The Case for Marriage, an important new book by Linda J. Waite and Maggie Gallagher, cohabitation's biggest attraction is the relatively easy exit with few responsibilities. Unfortunately, for many young adults, their parents' failed marriages may contribute to the expectation that marriages are fragile and divorce is common.

Those afraid of commitment and permanence, or who fear that these qualities can no longer be found in marriage, may settle for cohabitation. Only to discover, later, they have settled for much less. Cohabiting relationships are relatively short-lived- after five years, only about 10 percent of couples who cohabit and do not marry each other are still together.

Furthermore, those cohabiters who marry each other may be as much as 46 percent more likely to divorce than people who marry but have not cohabited first. The chances of commitment and permanence are better with marriage. Marriage is more likely to last than cohabitation even in the early years of the relationship. According to 1997 data, 14.5 percent of first marriages of women who had never cohabited ended in separation, divorce, or annulment in the first five years, compared to 22.6 percent of first marriages of women who had cohabited (with anyone) before those marriages.

Moreover, the breakup of a cohabiting relationship is not necessarily cleaner or easier than divorce. A breakup involves breaking up a household and may lead to conflicts over property, leases, past due bills, etc. Breaking up is emotionally difficult for both cohabiters and any children of their own or previous relationships. Women in their late twenties and thirties experience an additional loss-their biological clocks have been ticking while they cohabited; when they break up, they have lost valuable time in which to find a marriageable partner and have children.

Conclusion: In the final analysis, thirty years of research show that for the benefit of men, women, and their children, marriage is superior to cohabitation. Cohabitation cannot provide or compete with the rewards and benefits of a strong, committed marriage. Cohabitation is not an effective "trial marriage," if such a thing exists. It does not provide divorce insurance. Couples operate better on life's measures of success and happiness (e.g., emotional health, physical health, and personal wealth) if they marry rather than live together.

Cohabitation has many more costs than rewards: though many times not noticed nor discussed. Yet, unfortunately cohabitation continues to be popular, especially among young adults. Despite cohabiters failure to receive the benefits or avoid the risks they think might occur, it is a growing phenomena. The knowledge needs to be made known at home and abroad; "cohabitation fails to bring couples the happiness and stability they desire in a close personal relationship." Again the declaration is, "Marriage should be honored by all, and the marriage bed kept pure, for God will judge the adulterer and all the sexually immoral" (Hebrews 13: 4 NIV).

The effect of cohabitation on the children!

Be reminded, the practice of cohabitation is a device, designed by the devil and serves no Godly purpose for all parties involved. What about the children of cohabiters? They have issues too. American Values says, "Children of cohabiters are more likely than children of married parents to feel of worthless, nervous and tense. According to an article in Husbands and Dads:

"Cohabiting couples put their children at risk in the following ways: "According to the Journal of Marriage and Family, since cohabiting couples are more likely to break up than married couples, children are five times more likely to experience the breakup of their parents. Children are fifty times more likely to be abused when they are not living with two biological or adoptive parents, according to U.S. Census data.

Even factoring in socioeconomic and mental health differences, cohabiting couples' children are twice as likely to suffer from psychiatric disorders, diseases, suicide attempts, alcoholism, and drug abuse. They are more likely to suffer the negative effects of poverty and low socioeconomic status. They are more likely to have difficulties forming healthy relationships.

This list is a stunning condemnation of the effects of cohabitation on children. "In no published research is there any evidence that cohabitation is beneficial to the health and wellbeing of children." (Husband and Dad. com)

Just Wait 'Til Your Daddy Gets Home

Clearly, the evidence supports the position that cohabitation is a serious threat to marriage and the stability of the family unit. The most important advice that needs passing on is, "How to attain and maintain a loving family. Men note the following: If you want to be happy for the rest of your life, get a woman to be your wife. Not a roommate or someone to help pay the bills and sleep with, but a wife, men; and women, get a husband. This concept of God cannot be ignored. The entire civilization of mankind deeply depends upon it.

Beyonce has a point!

Normally, I don't quote nonreligious people (not to say that Beyonce is not religious; I don't know whether she is or not), but her music is not. Yet the song, "Put a Ring on it" has some merit. Young people, notice the message.

> Up in the club (club), we just broke up (up)I'm doing my own little thing, You decided to dip (dip), but now you want to trip (trip) Cause another brother noticed me I'm up on him (him), he up on me (me), Don't pay him any attentionCause I cried my tears (tears), for three good years (years). You can't be mad at me. Cause if you liked it then you should have put a ring on it.

The message is sung loud and clear, you should have married me, while you had the chance. Marriage is still the best chance of permanency.

Out of all the advice Beyonce has offered over the years through her music, the advice to have the young men marry their women seems to be the best. Granted, I am not an expert on the music of Beyonce, though at least one of my three daughters admires her greatly. However, on this point within this song, I hope and pray that her advice is accepted and applied. The Scripture still commands, "Marriage should be honored by all, and the marriage bed kept pure, for God will judge the adulterer and all the sexually immoral" (Hebrews 13: 4 NIV). Thus to attain and maintain a loving family, the importance of marriage, the two parent (husband and wife, male and female) presence in the home cannot be over stated.

Another step "To attain and maintain a loving family is for all involved to accept their God given roles. Man must recognize his leadership role and step up to it. The other members of the family must accept their role and that of the man's role as well. The Bible reveals all facts, including man was created in the image and "glory" of God (Genesis 1: 26-27 & I Cor. 11: 7). Therefore, God, the Father determines the role of man and the role of father. He also determined the role of the wife and mother. "Got questions .org put it this way concerning the wife and mother:

"Being a mother is a very important role that the Lord chooses to give to many women. A Christian mother is told to love her children (Titus 2:4-5), in part so that she does not bring reproach on the Lord and on the Savior whose name she bears. Children are a gift from the Lord (Psalm 127:3-5). In Titus 2:4, the Greek word philoteknos appears in reference to mothers loving their children. This word represents a special kind of "mother love." The idea flowing from this word consists of caring for our children, nurturing them, affectionately embracing them, meeting their needs, and tenderly befriending each one as a unique gift from the hand of God. Mothers take note:

Several things are commanded of mothers in God's Word: Availability – morning, noon, and night (Deuteronomy 6: 6-7).

Involvement – interacting, discussing, thinking, and processing life together (Ephesians 6:4)

Teaching – the Scriptures and a biblical worldview (Psalm 78:5-6; Deuteronomy 4:10; Ephesians 6:4)

Training – helping a child to develop skills and discover his/her strengths (Proverbs 22:6) and spiritual gifts (Romans 12:3-8 and 1 Corinthians 12)

Discipline – teaching the fear of the Lord, drawing the line consistently, lovingly, firmly (Ephesians 6:4; Hebrews 12:5-11; Proverbs 13:24; 19:18; 22:15; 23:13-14; 29:15-17)

Nurture – providing an environment of constant verbal support, freedom to fail, acceptance, affection, unconditional love (Titus 2:4; 2 Timothy 1:7; Ephesians 4:29-32; 5:1-2; Galatians 5:22; 1 Peter 3:8-9)

Modeling with Integrity – living what you say, being a model from which a child can learn by "catching" the essence of godly living (Deuteronomy 4:9, 15, 23; Proverbs 10:9; 11:3; Psalm 37:18, 37).

At the end of the description of an excellent wife, Proverbs 31 says: "Her children rise up and bless her; her husband also, and he praises her saying: "Many daughters have done nobly, but you excel them all." Charm is deceitful and beauty is vain, but a woman who loves the Lord shall be praised.

Correction, notice, the Bible never states that every woman should be a mother. It says, those whom the Lord blesses to be mothers should take the responsibility seriously. Mothers have a unique and crucial role in the lives of their children. Motherhood is not a chore or unpleasant task.

As mothers bear children during pregnancy, feeds and cares for them during infancy, they must play ongoing roles in the lives of their children. It does not matter whether or not; the children are adolescents, teenagers, young adults, or even adults with children of their own. The role of motherhood sometimes change and develops, yet the love, care, nurture, and encouragement a mother gives never ceases" (Gotquestions.org).

Also noted within the great marriages of the Bible and history, both the man and woman submitted themselves before God. It only makes sense, since he created them and their roles were determined and accepted by him for all within the family. It is the will of God that the husband and wife both acknowledge the man to be leader in matters of life.

On the ladder of authority and responsibility, man is one rung ahead of the woman. To any disputers, the scripture clarifies, "the husband is the head of his wife" (I Cor. 11: 3, Eph. 5: 22-24).

Man is to take the lead in the matter of religions (I Tim. 2: 8-15, contrast verses 8 and 9).

The husband is to love his wife as Christ loved the church and gave himself for it. This is no simple and easy suggestion. Christ loved the church enough to die and actually did die for it. He put his love into action. He said, "Greater love hath no man than this; that he lay down his life for his friends."

The husband (the head of his wife and family), must do the same. He is to love his wife enough to die for her. Which in actuality, clearly means, he is to put her welfare ahead of his own. To be the head is much more demanding than to be the neck (if you get my drift). The man is the head and the men that claim the right of headship, must also claim the right of sacrifice of self for her benefit. At the cash register of life, one cannot be claimed without the other. This is another necessary step in the attainment and maintenance of a loving family.

The Family man cannot be a loner.

God saw that it was not good that man be alone (Gen. 2: 18-20). God made a special companion for man (Gen. 2: 21-23). A "she-man" for the "he-man" (Hebrew, "woman") was made out of man: His Prime rib. God instituted marriage for man and woman (Gen. 2: 24, 25, "cleave unto his wife" is indicative of the commitment of marriage as opposed to cohabitation or shacking).

Again, make note: There is a sense of stability, longevity and security in marriage, not found in other relationships as seen above. Man is the provider (Gen. 3: 19, I Tim. 5: 8, & Tit. 2: 5. The Biblical woman is assistance and primarily responsible for the running of the household, Prov. 31: 16, 24).

The family man must be a lover ("He must love his wife and cleave unto her" (Gen. 2: 24, Matt. 19: 5, 6 & Eph. 5). He is to treat his wife in a certain way (Eph. 5: 25-31, I Pet. 3: 7). There is more to fatherhood than just being responsible for conception.

He is a leader in terms of learning and training. The father is presented in the Scriptures as also the leader in the area of training the children (Eph. 6: 4, 1, Prov. 4: 1-13). The Scriptures teach, to do before teach and preach. He must be a disciple (learner) himself.

He is a leader in terms of Godly living. Therefore, the father should first exemplify a Godly life (2 Cor. 3: 2).

He is the leading disciplinarian (Eph. 6: 4, Prov. 13: 24). He is to take a leadership role in teaching his children about God, the plan of salvation, the church, conviction and morals, and living the life of the Christian and general character development (Deut. 6: 6-9).

Conclusion: Out of all the roles a man may play in life (husband, coach, teacher, repairman, etc.), the role of father is the most fulfilling and cherished. As one grows older, the thoughts centering on fatherhood are the most cherished. In a popular television commercial, a mechanic says in reference to maintaining your automobile, "Pay me now or pay me later."

Also, this truth is evident in the area of raising children. Put in the time now with the children and there will be less troublesome time later. There's an old saying, "Children brought in Sunday school are seldom brought up in court."

Chapter VII
How To Attain And Maintain Loving Families, Part Two! What's Children Got To With It? Everybody's Has A Part To Play, Including The Children

"Children, obey your parents in the Lord, for this is right. Honor your father and mother (which is the first commandment with a promise), that it may be well with you, and that you may live long on the earth (Ephesians 6:1-3 kjv)."

The role given to children is very simple. They are to obey their parents. In view of actual practices within our society and those that exist within the church, it must be concluded that this scriptural directive has been forgotten or confused by the vast majority of parents. Within society, in regards to rearing children, there are some extremes that should be avoided. The Lord's commands need to be followed concerning the family and His wisdom, not the foolish wisdom of the world.

Get back to the basics!

The prevalent extreme in our society exits because there has been a basic change in our understanding of children and the way we view them. The majority of our nation no longer views children the way previous generations did. In particular, people's views are different today from those prior to the 1950s and early sixties. Back in the day, Americans were more Biblically literate. It was common place to see people doing evil, and the thought was that they did evil simply because people were considered evil and sinful by nature. There wasn't much complication about it; evil people perpetrated evil.

To restrain evil the thought was; people committing evil must be held accountable for their actions. Sin must be held in check. It was also known by the earlier generations, the only cure for sin was the gospel of Jesus Christ. Sin was, and is, cured only through faith in Jesus Christ and His atoning blood. It is through the work of the Holy Spirit that men and women are regenerated and sanctified which in affect changes the heart and practice of people.

Thus people and children are no longer held responsible for themselves. Today the problem is, many in society believe in the goodness of man, and that goodness comes from without rather from within: A false reality and sad state of affairs. In other words, many believe it is someone else's fault and others are always to blame, even for their sin. Be it poverty, drugs, sexual promiscuity or some other disorder.

What do children have to do with it?

Today's thinking about children assumes that they all are good people, though young and immature. If left alone and not interfered with or abused by somebody, they will grow up to be functioning adults. Remember Dr. Spock. His thought was, "You can't spoil a baby. His wants are his needs." Because of this advice, many made the child the center of attention within the family unit with everything focusing on meeting the children needs. Sadly, that ideology continues today.

The unfortunate results: Children out of control, ripping and running up and down church, store and home aisles without supervision. This behavior is terrible enough in the homes in which they live; but they have the audacity to bring it into everybody else's as well. There are too many children, misbehaving and refusing to do what grown folks tell them.

Even some children have the audacity to call parents out of their names or by their first names, and some even tell them to shut up and be quiet. While some parents want to be friends and think it is fine and dandy for the child to call them by their first name, they are deliberately destroying the separation between child and parent. Once torn down, it is almost impossible to be rebuilt.

Visiting, I've been in homes where the walls were heavily marked with crayon and holes and scars as high as the child is tall. As these children get older, the problems will increase, if not put in check. Teens will remain immature and self-centered. Some will no doubt become sociopaths with no concern for other people.

As stated before, children steal, lie and hurt other people because they are children and children are self-centered. They must be taught differently. They are "born in sin and shaped in iniquity" (Psalm 51: 5, KJV) and on the wrong path. Yet, it is the parent, not the child that has been given charge to direct them.

Notice the warning of Proverbs 20:20,"he who curses his father or his mother, His lamp will go out in time of darkness." 19:26, "He who assaults his father and drives his mother away is a shameful and disgraceful son." 29:15 "The rod and reproof give wisdom, but a child who gets his own way brings shame to his mother." 30:17, "The eye that mocks a father, and scorns a mother, the ravens of the valley will pick it out, and the young eagles will eat it" (NIV).

Parents gone too far

There's another extreme in parenting practice that is not as common as it used to be, but still, it can be found. This view does not place children at the center of the family. But rather, it places the father not as the head of the family, but king. Mother may or may not be reigning as queen, but clearly, the children are not where they should be.

In this view, love and nurture takes a back seat to keeping the law. Punishment comes swiftly, and many times the punishment doesn't fit the crime. There is an even sadder side of things; many times Scripture is used to justify injustice and abuse.

This style of parenting leaves the child existing only for the benefit of the parent. When the child intrudes on the parent's lifestyle through childishness or misbehavior, severe consequences are handed down. Fear becomes the child's motivation for action. Fear of parents, fear of God and subsequently fear of all authority figures. Children soon develop prohibitive consciences. Their lives are seen in terms of restrictions and "Thou shalt not."

The child is governed and appreciated only by what is seen on the outside and while they may exhibit exemplary discipline and ethical behavior, on the inside the child may be completely missing the mark. The tragedy is, when the children become adults, many end up with a distorted picture of God. Remember God warn parents, "not to provoke their children to anger" (Eph. 6:4) and to "not exasperate [them] that they may not lose heart" (Col. 3:20).

It should not surprise anyone that some children grow up in homes with training; they will reject. Many supposedly "good kids" get buck wild when they go to college or just leave home for the first time. Mom and Dad's rules and regulations are at home with them. The time away at college is for them to live how they want and demonstrate and develop their own beliefs. The only avenue for parents is to teach and preach the best they can, while they have the attention of the young. When they leave the nest, unless the heart is changed, they will rebel.

Stay in the middle of the road. How do we avoid the extremes of life and keep things in the middle of the road. It begins with the knowledge of knowing the purpose and role of all persons within the family unit. The roles of the father and mother have been addressed, now attention turn toward the children. Here's where and how to begin.

Continuation of mankind! Genesis 1:28. God told Adam and Eve to "Be fruitful and multiply, and fill the earth." The way man lives, he is always just one generation away from extinction.

Continuation of the knowledge of God. Israel was to pass their knowledge of God from one generation unto the next.

Deut. 6:4 "Hear, O Israel! The Lord is our God, the Lord is one! "And you shall love the Lord your God with all your heart and with all your soul and with all your might. "And these words, which I am commanding you today, shall be on your heart; and you shall teach them diligently to your sons and shall talk of them when you sit in your house and when you walk by the way and when you lie down and when you rise up.

Psalm 78:5 For He established a testimony in Jacob, And appointed a law in Israel, Which He commanded our fathers, That they should teach them to their children, That the generation to come might know, [even] the children [yet] to be born, [That] they may arise and tell [them] to their children, that they should put their confidence in God, And not forget the works of God, But keep His commandments. Again notice Eph. 6:4–"...bring them up in the discipline and instruction of the Lord.

It is not being declared that people cannot come to the knowledge of Christ because of their parent's beliefs. If that was the case, the Great Commission is null and void, even a lie. The church was and is to proclaim the gospel message to everyone. The Lord in His graciousness saves people. Only remember Acts 1:8, it declares the mission to begin in Jerusalem, the home ground of the missionary. So, parents must realize, their first priority in evangelism and discipleship is to their own children within their home.

One of the tragic mistakes that many pastors make is, they think, if they take care of the church, the church in turn will take care of their families, if something happens negatively to them. Many children turn away from Christ because dad has not been home long enough to model Christ to them. According to Scripture, such men are actually unqualified to Pastor, 1Timothy 3 and Titus 1. Matthew 16: 13-18, Jesus said, He would build His church.

While He uses people to accomplish the goal, the priority placed upon all of us, was and is to raise our children in His nurture and admonition. Note: God gave children in order that parents may pass their knowledge and understanding of God on to them, in order to build upon the foundation that is already laid.

Another purpose of children is to be a blessing. Psalm 127:3-5, "Behold, children are a gift of the Lord; the fruit of the womb is a reward. Like arrows in the hand of a warrior, so are the children of one's youth. How blessed is the man whose quiver is full of them; they shall not be ashamed, When they speak with their enemies in the gate."

Children are blessings from God. They bring so much into life. There are many heartaches and tough days of raising children but they bring such joy. Children love life. They wonder at the world around them and are happy over such simple pleasures.

Yet, notice one of the real blessings of life is the teaching about trusting and walking with the Lord. It teaches to think less of personal wants and teaches more to love sacrificially. Children will reflect parents and allow the world an open door to their lives.

Through the eyes of the children, people are allowed to view both the good and bad in parents, thus hopefully prods the parent to greater holiness. The presence of children should cause more careful actions and people should take note of what is said and done, but also what is thought. There's no doubt, children are blessings from God to us and how we treat them is our response to God. Love them and show God that we appreciate his gifts.

Children will be children. To understand the role of children, we must remember their position within the family. They are not the center of the family as in the "anything goes" philosophy of today. Neither are they somewhere on the outskirts in orbit as happens in other philosophies. Children are a key part of the family.

So, what is it that children have to do to attaining and maintaining a loving family? With each new life added to your family is another precious soul for you to teach about God and guide directly into eternity. Children bring out the best in man. They are so vulnerable and trusting and were put in our lives for us to teach them. As said repeatedly in the book, one of the parent's main responsibilities is to teach them. The children's responsibility is to learn.

Paul commanded the man to lead his wife in sanctification so that she might be holy and blameless. The same is true for children. Their role is to learn from both husband and wife the identity of God, His attributes and how to have a personal relationship with Him.

Reiterating, the father's role primarily is to teach. The children's is to learn and learning begins with obedience. In the olden days, the schoolmaster was sometime needed to help shape the child's behavior, character and belief system. Proper obedience leads to the freedom of living, positively out of love for righteousness, rather than living in fear of doing wrong.

Children, listen up!

The child's first and foremost responsibility in the family is to obey the parent. Here, the word "obey" literally means, "To hear under," and also includes the idea of hearing and responding positively. Attitude as well as action is important in obedience. If you grumble or whine about what you are asked to do, you are not obeying even if you do what you were told.

Listen to Paul, "Do everything without grumbling or arguing, so that you may become blameless and pure, "children of God without fault in a warped and crooked generation." Then you will shine among them like stars in the sky as you hold firmly to the word of life. And then I will be able to boast on the day of Christ that I did not run or labor in vain" (Phil. 2: 14-16, NIV).

Proverbs 6: 20, states, "My son, observe the commandment of your father, And do not forsake the teaching of your mother". This is not some conspiracy against you so that your life will be miserable, but rather God's commandment so that there will be order in the home and your life will be filled with blessings. Learning obedience to your parents is the first step toward learning obedience to the Lord, toward gaining self-control, and becoming considerate to the interests of others.

Self-control and considering the interests of other people are both vital to your getting along and becoming successful adults. Self-control is one of the foundational skills for learning, both mentally and physically. Without mental self-control, no one is able to focus attention, even to read, study, or analyze and solve problems. Every subject studied takes concentration, whether Math, History, Language, Art, Science and especially the Bible. The better your mental self-preparedness; the better performance can be done in all studies, regardless of intelligence.

Without physical self-control and self-preparedness, the skills needed to perform any kind of job will not be gained. It takes practice to learn to control ones fingers in order to nimbly use a keyboard to operate a computer. If control of ones hands cannot be contained, even a nail will not be driven properly, not to mention a power saw. The ability to speak requires precise control of vocal cords, tongue and lips. Clear communication requires a controlled mind otherwise what is said will not make sense.

Also, obedience is the foundation of consideration for other people. Obedience battles selfishness because it requires the containment of the will and putting it the authority of another. You are placed in a secondary position. If selfishness is allowed to live, a lack of concern for other people will fester and bring nothing but problems in life.

Permit me to demonstrate the importance of this by a simple question? Do you like being around self-centered people who give no consideration to your thoughts or feelings? How do you respond to people, you come into contact with in the business world, church or community whose interest in you is only money?

Parents must teach obedience as a prerequisite for children obeying God and others, teachers, law enforcement, etc. The first lessons taught about consequences came from parents. Parents must teach; disobedience brings punishment while obedience brings blessings.

Children who refuse simple instructions from parents while physically present with them will have serious problems later, obeying God whom they cannot physically behold. The lesson is a far better one, if the child learns early while the consequences are only spankings or withholding of privileges rather than the wrath of God.

Again, the primary role of children is obedience and that begins with it the foundation of learning. The commandment is; "obey your father and mother and live long on the land that the Lord God hath given thee." The commandment is a serious one. The result of disobeying God's commandments is sin and the loss of blessings. Parents, who allow such behavior are sinning themselves and at the same time, train, the child to sin.

The command of God to obey your parents is not an option. The consequences of disobedience are devastating. Separation from God and eternity in Hell is devastating enough by itself, but the other losses of health, prosperity and long life on the earth makes it even more so.

The limitations. There are limitations. The commandment reads, "Children are to obey their parents in the Lord." In all situations where one person is under authority, no matter whose or what the authority, it must be understood, children's first allegiance is to the Lord. When there is conflict, the Lord must be obeyed rather than man, including parents. At times, it may cause some serious consequences but children must not violate God's commandments for anything or person.

Neither can children lie, steal, kill, bare false witness, etc. even for parents. In no ways can they assist them in committing sin. When faced with the temptation, they must respectfully decline and remind the parent of the commands of God. Suffering is a part of Christianity for all followers, including children.

It must be remembered, Jesus Christ, the prophets and apostles all suffered for righteousness sake. Though, the good news is, the story does not conclude with suffering. Paul said, "I have fought a good fight, I have finished my course, I have kept the faith: Henceforth there is laid up for me a crown of righteousness, which the Lord, the righteous judge, shall give me at that day: and not to me only, but unto all them also that love his appearing" (II Tim. 4: 7kjv).

The tragedy is that some parents ask children to lie, steal, bare false witness, and even kill for them. They often tell children to answer the phone or the door and say, they are not home. Children should say respectfully, you will have to do it. Or tell the person at the door, "Momma or Dad, do not want to be disturbed right now; can you call or come back later?"

Some parents have been known to tell the children to lie about their age so parents can get a discount at dinner or the theater, etc. Children, remind the parent of God's commands, not to lie or steal. "Children obey your parents, but obey them in the Lord" as the commands accurately state.

Parents must be parents first and friends second. (Those that do deserve honor.)

In Eph. 6: 3- 4, Paul repeats Exodus 20: 12 from the Ten Commandments. This is the basis for his conclusions in verse number one. "Honor your father and mother that it may be well with you, and that you may live long on the earth." Paul informs that this is the first commandment with a promise. He reminds man that there are blessings in obeying and serving the Lord. In this commandment God says specifically what they are. "Honor your parents and not only will life go well, there will be long life on the earth."

The promise is both general and specific. In the general sense, a person who has learned obedience also has learned the skills needed to have a good life. They go together. As has already been mentioned self-control and consideration of others are the keys to good relationships.

Thus generally, the natural consequence of honoring your parents and the skills learned from doing so, lead to a good life. A good life of health and strength usually leads to a long life. It makes sense that one leads to the other.

On the other hand, sin (which incorporates fast and foolish living) characteristically cuts off life. Similarly, to those who operate justly in their everyday business lives promises are also made (Deut. 25: 15). As is to those who are wise (Prov. 3: 16) and keep God's commandments (Deut. 4:40; 32:47).

These are direct promises of God; as the blessing to those who honor their father and mother. This does not mean that God cannot and will not bless others for different reasons. For example, believers who are persecuted for trusting Christ (such as Daniel, the three Hebrew believers and others) have the promise of long life and specifically those who honor father and mother.

Of course, one of the rewards for obedience to God is blessings. In fact, the prophet Samuel asked a significant question on the subject. I Sam 15:22, says, "And Samuel said, hath the Lord as great delight in burnt offerings and sacrifices, as in obeying the voice of the LORD? Behold, to obey is better than sacrifice, and to hearken than the fat of rams" (KJV).

An examination of the commandment to honor the Lord primarily means "to place value upon:" To respect and consider. Regardless of age, race, denomination, all humans are to demonstrate respect and consideration to their parents. This is how young people are to honor their parents; through obedience and submission to them.

It does not matter if one is eighty years of age; they are to honor their parents. Children are to willingly follow the instruction and advice of their parents. This is done out of love and devotion to them. The schoolmaster of obedience has been the teacher that has taught them submission.

Adulthood and independent living may change the authority and submission issue, since the adult no longer resides with their parent, but honor and respect never changes. The Scripture teaches men to leave father and mother and cleave unto the wife. It teaches women, the husband is now the head of the family, no longer the father.

Having said that, it still needs saying again, adults are still to give honor and respect to our parents. This is done by visitation, listening, loving and honoring them. It is a joy to love, respect and honor parents that have sacrificed and done so much in the raising of the young. Honor stems from the innate appreciation that was birth of devotion. Good parents deserve respect, appreciation and care from the children.

On the other hand, unfortunately, all parents have not been good. There have been some uncaring and abusive. There have been children who have suffered deeply at their parent's doing. Their history is full of pain and agony. The trust they placed in mom and dad was broken back then and the current relationship isn't much better.

Although regardless of the past, children must still honor the parent. Even if only just to never speak evil of them; degrade them, deny them food and shelter or ignore them in time of need. The Scripture demands that we do as much for our enemies, less knowing for our parents.

Remember all are commanded to love their neighbor as themselves (Mk. 12: 31 KJV). The danger in not obeying the commands of God to love is that we lose just as much as others. It must be interjected, the Scripture declares, "if we forgive men NOT their trespasses, God will not forgive us ours" (Matthew 6: 15, KJV). At the least, children should honor their parent out of love for Jesus Christ and commitment to obey Him.

Finally, the children's role is to obey their parents in the Lord. Parents are to teach them about God, the world, and the rest of His creation. They are to be taught how to live in obedience to

Him. Godly children are not born godly, they must be taught and trained up in the way that they should go and when they are old, they will not depart from it" (Proverbs 22: 6, KJV).

Those that desire godly children need to teach them to be so. Remember though, Jesus said teaching begins by example and at home first. So, teach by living the life yourself. Surely, God is worth our efforts to make the world a better place to live.

Please stay tuned to chapter VIII for the final instructions of the book, "Just wait 'til your daddy get home." If for any of the reasons listed above, one finds him/herself without a father coming home, all is not lost, there is still hope. Don't give up and miss the instructions and directions from the next chapter, "A Father of the Fatherless."

Chapter VIII
Father Of The Fatherless! What To Do When Daddy Doesn't Come Home! Make the Best out of a Bad situation!

"Father of the fatherless and protector of widows is God in his holy habitation" (Psalm 68: 5, ESV).

But Jesus said, Suffer little children, and forbid them not, to come unto me: for of such is the kingdom of heaven" (Matt.19: 14 KJV).

"Five fatherless daughters in the wilderness" (Number 27: 3).

"Abraham's father dies" (Genesis 11 & Acts 7: 4).

On the subject of making the best out of a bad situation, the author speaks with personal experience. Please, allow the strong suggestions and a few recommendations to the children found numbered among the fatherless. The state in which you find yourself is highly unfortunate and certainly, undeserved. Know that the misfortune in which you find yourself is not your fault. Categorically, in no way, shape or form, are you to blame for the desertion of young and adult care takers. The responsibility for your condition lie elsewhere, so lift up your heads.

Further, here is some additional good news. The state of your present situation, no matter how dark and dismal is not the end of the story. You must have faith and believe that it is just one chapter in the mega book of life. There will be plenty other chapters written before the final ending is told. There are plenty of personal testimonies. I am a living and testifying witness telling you categorically, you will make it, if you try. God's word is on the line. He has promised to be a father to the fatherless, and as the songwriter said, "He has never failed me yet." Success is his business.

Note his word.

"A Father of the fatherless and Protector of the widows is God in his holy habitation." In the wilderness of Mt. Sinai, the people were like orphans. But God was more than a father to them. As the generation that came out of Egypt gradually died, there were many widows and fatherless in the camp.

However, they suffered no want or injustice. The righteous laws and just administrators appointed by God looked out for the interests of the needy and the less fortunate. Those without biological fathers and mothers, God provided protection and provision. Such was the case in Numbers 27: 3. "Five fatherless daughters in the wilderness"

Remember in the ancient world, a father's property was divided among his sons. The oldest son received twice as much as the younger sons. Daughters did not receive property. Rather, when they were married, they received a dowry or a wedding present from their father. Of course, what they received depended upon the wealth of the father. Wealthy fathers were known to give large dowries such as expensive clothing, jewelry, perfumes, money, furniture, slave-help, and sometimes even houses and entire cities.

Once the daughter had married, the father had no more responsibility for her, and she received no inheritance of land or property upon his death. By law she became a full-fledged member of the family into which she married.

Exactly this was the deep concern that gripped the hearts of these five dear sisters in Numbers 27: 3, the daughters of Zelophehad. The outline of the Scripture states very simply the terms of the injustice they were feeling; No doubt an injustice that existed with other women throughout history and the nation.

The father of the dear sisters died leaving no sons, only them as the surviving members of the family. The Scripture noted, he died believing in the Promised Land as delivered by Moses, not in Korah's rebellion that sought to replace Moses and to lead the

Israelites back to Egypt. Their father had been a true believer in God's promises: he had not been a seeker of the pleasures of Egypt nor of this world.

The faith of these five daughters in the Promised Land of God was strong. Apparently their plea and appeal touched the hearts of the judges and members of the Supreme Court hearing their case. They wanted their father's name and the testimony of his faith in the Lord preserved. Therefore, they requested his inheritance (Numbers 27:4). They asked the Supreme Court remember their father's name. Why should his name disappear from the history books and he lose his identity? Should all of this be done just because he had no sons?

Here the point is being made of the great faith and hope, the women had in God and His Promised Land. It needs to be remembered that Israel had not entered the Promised Land, yet these dear women had faith in God and his justice and care. They knew that God was going to lead the Israelites into the Promised Land and there, the Israelites would be given their inheritance. God keeping his word was not a question to them. They were women of deep conviction, faith, and hope in the great inheritance promised by God.

Their faith was strong enough to do something that had never been done in the history of the Israelite Nation. They appeared before the supreme court of the land to change one of the most basic and ancient laws in history: a history dominated by men from the foundation of the world. The law of question was the law of inheritance or of the birthright, a law that gave the inheritance of land only to the sons of a family.

But these dear women believed God's promise of the Promised Land, but also believed in God's other attributes as well. The Scripture says, He is a "Father of the fatherless and protector of widows is God in his holy habitation" (Psalm 68: 5, ESV).

They believed it, so much so that they were willing to risk everything in order to secure their inheritance. They wanted the godly heritage and inheritance of their family's name to be carried on through succeeding generations. They wanted the inheritance that their father had both lived and died for.

Numbers 27: 7, informs us that Moses took their case before the Lord. God ordered Moses to both protect and provide for the fatherless children. He was to give them their father's inheritance and change the law of the land to insure that if the fatherless children were orphaned, they would be provided for forever. God is father to the fatherless.

This is one of the reasons the tabernacle was the "Palace of Justice;" the Ark of the Covenant was the seat of the great King. The Children of Israel were blessed and there was cause for great joy. They were ruled by the One God that would not suffer the poor and needy to be oppressed. Still, to this day and forever, God is; and always will be the Protective guardian of the defenseless. It could even be said, God is the true President of Orphanages and Protector of Widows.

Think about it, the God we serve is so glorious and awesome that he rides on the heavens, but at the same time, so humble and compassionate that he remembers every poor soul in the earth. How zealously should his Church also cherish those who are here marked out as God's "Special Needs Children?"

Did God not ask Peter three times, if you love me, "Feed my sheep?" It is mankind's blessed duty and privilege to make His mission, their mission. Be careful here not to misquote the verse. Many times; it is misquoted to read, "God is the husband of the widow," but Scripture says, "He's a father to the fatherless and protector of the widows." It's best to be left as God gave it.

To further define a father of the fatherless, or father of orphans. Compare Psalm 10:14, Psalm 10:18. That is, God takes the place of the parent. See Jeremiah 49:11 : "Leave thy fatherless children, I will preserve them alive; and let thy widows trust in me." This is one of the tender appellations that could be given to God, and conveys one of the most striking descriptions of his character.

We see his greatness, his majesty, his power, in the worlds that he has made—in the storm, the tempest, the rolling ocean; but it is in such expressions as this that we learn, what we most desire to know, and what we cannot elsewhere learn, that he is a Father; that he is to be loved as well as feared.

Nothing suggests more strikingly a state of helplessness and dependence than the condition of orphan children and widows; nothing, therefore, conveys a more affecting description of the character of God—of his condescension and kindness—than to say that he will take the place of the parent in the one case, and be a protector in the other.

And a judge of the widows—That is, He will see justice done them; he will save them from oppression and wrong. There are no persons more liable to be oppressed and wronged than widows. They are regarded as incapable of defending or vindicating their own rights. They are likely to be deceived and betrayed by those to whom their property and rights may be entrusted.

Hence, the care which God manifests for them, his solemn charges, so often made to those who are in authority, and who are entrusted with power, to respect their rights; hence, his frequent and solemn rebukes to those who violate their rights. See the notes at Isaiah 1:17. Compare Deuteronomy 10:18; Deuteronomy 14:29; Deuteronomy 24:17; Exodus 22:22; Job 24:3, Job 24:21; Jeremiah 7:6; Malachi 3:5; James 1:27.

Is God in his holy habitation—Where he dwells; in heaven? The design of the psalmist seems to take man, once summoned up to God and let man see what he is in his holy home. Also, how he is to conduct himself in his presence, that we may see him as he is.

This is the idea here, if God is approached humbly and looked upon not merely in the splendor and magnificence of his appearance, nor how he governs the worlds, in terms of his judgments, or how he operates in the storms and tempest, rides on the clouds and controls the ocean, but, simply as he dwells in heaven, he would be discovered.

The closer his character is looked upon, it will be found that his character is best represented by the kind and benignant traits of a father in his care for orphans and widows. In simpler words, the more God is seen, the more intimately acquainted with his real nature is revealed- the more evidence is found that he is benevolent and kind.

Psalm 68:5. 'Leave thy fatherless children, I will preserve them alive; And let thy widows trust in me." (Psalm 68: 5 KJV).

The Biblical conclusion of the matter!

"A father of the fatherless:" literally means to show mercy, take care of and protect. This is a character which the great God often assumes, partly to express his power and providence and partly to signify his tenderness, mercy, and goodness. It would be of great significance if God would be imitated by civil magistrates and by all good men. It was not only a law in Israel to show regard to such, and take care not to afflict, but also a branch of pure undefiled Christian religion, James 1:27.

Moreover, this may be understood in a spiritual sense for those deserted by their friends, or those called to leave father and mother for the sake of Christ and his Gospel. Those fatherless and helpless who will not trust in the creature or in any works of their own, but apply their hearts to Christ will be rewarded. In him, "they have help and salvation and mercy being fatherless" (Hosea 14:3).

Any found without the presence of Christ and sensible communion with him are like orphans or fatherless children. Yet through Christ, the father of such children will not leave them, but have pity on them. He will show them favor and provide everything needful for them. He will come and visit them, John 14:18; described the word "orphans" or "fatherless," in reference to Christ's disciples. God is The Father of the fatherless.

The Father of the faithful, father died

"And the days of Terah were two hundred and five years: and Terah died in Haran" (Genesis 11: 32, KJV).

Finally, Abraham the founding Father of the Nation of Israel and one of the great personalities of the Bible was tremendously blessed after the death of his father. Note the below:

Abraham was born in Ur of Chaldees in 2166 B, C. He married Sarai and migrated to Haran with his cousin Lot and Father, Terah. Terah died in Haran (Genesis 11). The Lord commanded Abram to leave Haran and travel to Canaan. On arriving there, he traveled as far as Schechem to the center of the Promised Land and the whole of the land would be his possession. From there, he went to Bethel and built a second altar to the Lord.

In the year, 2091, Abram departed from Haran and arrived in Canaan. Because of the famine, he took the family down to Egypt. He deceived Pharaoh by passing his wife off as his sister. One thing led another and he became wealthy. After the lied was made known, Pharaoh sent them away (Genesis 12).

Abraham returned to Canaan traveling from the Negev in the South as far as Bethel. There he and Lot separated. Abraham allowed Lot to choose the better land. Yet God blessed Abraham more. After Lots departure the Lord, the Lord renews his promise of the land and thus Abraham moved his headquarters to Hebron where he built a third altar (Gen 13).

Now Lot has moved into Sodom and is captured by the forces of four invading kings and carried off. Abram musters his household and some local allies, pursues and defeats the invading kings and rescues Lot. On returning he is met by Melchizedek, King of Salem who **blesses him in the name of the Most High God. Abram accepts the blessing and gives Melchizedek a tenth of the plunder.**

Shortly afterwards the king of Sodom greets Abram to bless him, but Abram refuses to keep any of his property (Gen. 14). The Lord reassures Abram that the promises he has made will be fulfilled by means of a covenant ceremony (Gen. 15).

In the year 2081, Abraham married Hagar at the request of Sarai. The text says Sarai suggests that Abram take her maidservant Hagar and have children by her. Hagar conceives and Sarai becomes jealous of her. Fleeing from Sarai's mistreatment, Hagar meets the angel of the Lord at a spring in the desert and persuades her to return, promising that she would have a son named Ishmael who would be the father of a nation (Gen. 16). Thus God blesses Abram again.

In 2080, the birth of Ishmael. For the next 13 years, after the birth of Ishmael, the Scripture is silent about the events of Abram's life. At the age of 99, the Lord gave Abram the covenant of circumcision and changed his name from Abram (*exalted father*) to Abraham (*father of many*). Sarai was blessed as well, to now be known as Sarah. Also she would bear Abraham a son and heir, named, Isaac (Gen. 17).

The destruction the Sodom and Gomorrah in 2067: The events are recorded as follows: "The Lord and two angels visit Abraham and said Sarah would have a child of her own within the next year. He also informed Abraham that Sodom and the other cities of the plain were about to be dealt with for their wickedness. Abraham pleaded for Sodom and the Lord promised to spare the city if there were found ten righteous men there (Gen. 18).

The two angels went down to Sodom and were invited by Lot to sleep in his house. During the night the men of Sodom demand that Lot turn the angels over to them. At which point, the angels blinded the attackers and took Lot, his wife and their two daughters out of the city just before the Lord destroyed it.

Lot was the only righteous man in the city (Gen. 19). Abraham moved his camp into the territory of Abimelech king of Gerar, again pretending that Sarah was his sister. Abimelech takes Sarah as his wife but is prevented from committing adultery by a dream. Abimelech summons Abraham and after receiving an explanation from him for his conduct he gives him gifts of money, sheep and cattle and returns Sarah to him (Gen. 20). These are but a few of the many blessings God gave Abraham after the death of his father.

There is no doubt left that God is a "Father of the fatherless and protector of widows is God in his holy habitation" (Psalm 68: 5 ESV). If you have no earthly father in your life to speak of, consider God. He has many witnesses that there is no father like him. I vow to you that he will do you great.

Chapter IX
Children Caught In The Middle
Stop The Fighting (For The Children's Sake!)

The term "Caught in the middle" at the very least suggest awkwardness and discomfort. At the very most suggests pain, suffering and serious injury. Yet the term appropriately and accurately describes the predicament of children of warring parents.

The research and statistics support the reality of the devastation that children caught in the middle of conflict between the people they love the most deal with. A research article reveals, "Children from divorced families are caught in the middle of parental conflicts significantly more often and experience more stress than children from intact homes." Kurkowski, K., Gordon, D.A., & Arbuthnot, J. (1993).

Another article from the Anti-Divorce Revolution details the following interesting information: 70 % of divorces end "low-conflict" marriages! "Wallerstein and others who stress the high cost of divorce raise hackles among those committed to the view that children are better off when a bad marriage ends. But a new study of family upheaval by sociologists Paul Amato of the University of Nebraska and Alan Booth of Pennsylvania State University underlines some important distinctions. According to their research, reported in their 1997 book A Generation at Risk, the worst situations for children are high-conflict marriages that last and low-conflict marriages that end in divorce.

It turns out that most divorces fall into the latter category: A whopping 70 percent of divorces end "low-conflict" marriages. "For children's sake," Amato and Booth conclude, "some marriages should not be salvaged. But in marriages that are not fraught with severe conflict and abuse, future generations would be well served if parents remained together until children are grown." "The Anti-Divorce Revolution" in the Weekly Standanrd, Dec. 1997, http://www.smartmarriages.com/weeklystandard.html.

This article renews a bold conclusion that was commonly held by many of the previous generations. For some marriages, it is good for them to remain intact, although the marriage may not be the best or even considered great. As stated in the report, if there is no abuse, either physical or mental and the conflicts between husband and wife are minimal, in consideration of the disastrous consequences for the children of separated and divorced parents, the recommendation of the experts is for the husband and wife to remain together.

Husbands and wives make note: if there is no abuse, either physical or mental and the conflicts between husband and wife are minimal, the recommendation of the experts is for the husband and wife to remain together.

By now, the position of the author of this book should be clear and hopefully rightly interpreted that it is good for husbands and fathers to come home. Yet, there may be a need for some clarification on the point. If so, here it is. It is not being suggested that all men and husbands are good people.

Neither is it being suggested that every father should come home. Clearly, there are fathers and men in general that should not come home and be with their children or no one else's either. As in the case with LL Cool J's dad, he grew up with an abusive father. As did Charlize Theron, he grew up with an abusive and alcoholic father according to "Without a dad.com."

Those that mentally or physically abuse their wives or children should be removed from the premises. Men that take advantage of others living in the home by not working or contributing to the expenses and welfare of the family, yet, eat and drink everything in sight need not come home.

Men incapable of demonstrating love and affection, cold hearted and cold minded men, stay clear. Physically and mentally controlling men who want to control others but cannot control their out of control jealousy need not come home. Wives and children deserve better. The experts say, these are the type of relationships that need dissolving.

Although, prior to the 1960's; marriages lasted longer. In fact during those days divorce was highly unusual. The family's social structure was more rigid, as the roles of men and women were better defined and less easily challenged. Men went to work and women for the most part stayed home and cared for the children.

Few women had the wherewithal (economically, or emotionally) to walk away from unhappy marriages. There weren't any social assistance as today, so if the woman left, she would often find herself along and financially disabled. By the same token, the Morales of society held the male role of patriarch to provide for the family. As a result, there were less deadbeat dads walking the streets.

There was also another factor for families remaining together. In many cases, people did so for the children's wellbeing. As a result of this, criminality and corruption were very low during these times.. Particularly so, in comparison to the times we live in today. Needless to say, going back to some of the old ways would be highly beneficial, especially for the children.

Note: "Constance Ahrons's 1994 book The Good Divorce is a decidedly optimistic account of middle-class divorced couples. Yet she found that just 12 percent of divorced parents are able to create friendly, low-conflict relationships after divorce. Fifty percent of middle-class divorced couples engage in bitter, open conflict as "angry associates," or worse, "fiery foes." Five years afterwards, most of these angry divorced [couples] remain mired in hostility. Nearly a third of friendly divorces degenerate into open, angry conflict." Gallagher in "End No-Fault Divorce?"

Stop the fighting for the children's sake.

Women, listen up!

It has been said by William Congreve; "Heaven has no rage like love to hatred turned /nor hell's fury like a woman scorned." Also, it has been said," When Mom's happy everybody's happy, but when dad's unhappy, who cares? These are two of the more popular phrases being stated today, yet neither flatters the woman. It is not good for women to strive to be Divas; they should strive to be devoted mothers. There is so much at stake for the children. It should and must be about the children.

For the sake of the children, mothers give fathers that care the opportunity to participate in their lives. The children are the beneficiaries when daddies are present. Put your emotions aside and do the right thing for the children. Don't you be counted among these uncaring statistics!

- 37.9 percent of fathers have no access/visitation rights. (Source: p.6, col.II, para. 6, lines 4 & 5, Census Bureau P-60, #173, Sept 1991.)
- "40 percent of mothers reported that they had interfered with the non-custodial father's visitation on at least one occasion, to punish the ex-spouse." (Source: p. 449, col. II, lines 3-6, (citing Fulton) Frequency of visitation by Divorced Fathers; Differences in Reports by Fathers and Mothers. Sanford Braver et al, Am. J. of Orthopsychiatry, 1991.)
- "Overall, approximately 50 percent of mothers "see no value in the father`s continued contact with his children...." (Source: Surviving the Breakup, Joan Kelly & Judith Wallerstein, p. 125)
- Only 11 percent of mothers value their husband's input when it comes to handling problems with their kids. Teachers & doctors rated 45 percent, and close friends & relatives rated 16 percent. (Source: EDK Associates survey of 500 women for Redbook Magazine. Redbook, November 1994, p. 36)

- "The former spouse (mother) was the greatest obstacle to having more frequent contact with the children." (Source: Increasing our understanding of fathers who have infrequent contact with their children, James Dudley, Family Relations, Vol. 4, p. 281, July 1991.
- "The former spouse (mother) was the greatest obstacle to having more frequent contact with the children." (Source: Increasing our understanding of fathers who have infrequent contact with their children, James Dudley, Family Relations, Vol. 4, p. 281, July 1991.)
- "A clear majority (70 percent) of fathers felt that they had too little time with their children." (Source: Visitation and the Noncustodial Father, Mary Ann Kock & Carol Lowery, Journal of Divorce, Vol. 8, No. 2, p. 54, Winter 1984.)
- "Very few of the children were satisfied with the amount of contact with their fathers, after divorce." (Source: Visitation and the Noncustodial Father, Koch & Lowery, Journal of Divorce and Remarriage, Vol. 8, No. 2, p. 50, Winter 1984.)
- "Feelings of anger towards their former spouses hindered effective involvement on the part of fathers; angry mothers would sometimes sabotage father's efforts to visit their children." (Source: Ahrons and Miller, Am. Journal of Orthopsychiatry, Vol. 63. p. 442, July `93.)
- "Mothers may prevent visits to retaliate against fathers for problems in their marital or post-marital relationship." (Source: Seltzer, Shaeffer & Charing, Journal of Marriage & the Family, Vol. 51, p. 1015, November 1989.)
- In a study: "Visitational Interference–A National Study" by Ms. J Annette Vanini, M.S.W. and Edward Nichols, M.S.W., it was found that 77 percent of non-custodial fathers are NOT able to "visit" their children, as ordered by the court, as a result of "visitation interference"

perpetuated by the custodial parent. In other words, non-compliance with court ordered visitation is three times the problem of non-compliance with court ordered child support and impacts the children of divorce even more. (Originally published Sept. 1992)

Mothers, just for your information: the issue of child support:

- Information from multiple sources show that only 10 percent of all noncustodial fathers fit the "deadbeat dad" category: 90 percent of the fathers with joint custody paid the support due. Fathers with visitation rights pay 79.1 percent; and 44.5 percent of those with no visitation rights still financially support their children. (Source: Census Bureau report. Series P-23, No. 173).
- Additionally, of those not paying support, 66 percent are not doing so because they lack the financial resources to pay (Source: GAO report: GAO/HRD-92-39 FS).
- 52 percent of fathers who owe child support earn less than $6,155 per year. (Source: The Poverty Studies Institute at the University of Wisconsin, Madison, 1993)
- 66 percent of single mothers work less than full time while only 10 percent of fathers fall into this category. In addition, almost 47 percent of non-custodial mothers default on support compared with the 27 percent of fathers who default. (Source: Garansky and Meyer, DHHS Technical Analysis Paper No. 42, 1991).
- 66 percent of all support not paid by non-custodial fathers is due to inability to pay. (Source: U.S. General Accounting Office Report, GAO/HRD-92-39FS January 1992).
- Total Custodial Mothers: 11,268,000
- Total Custodial Fathers: 2,907,000 (Source: Current Population Reports, U.S. Bureau of the Census, Series P-20, No. 458, 1991).

- The following is sourced from: Technical Analysis Paper No. 42, U.S. Department of Health and Human Services, Office of Income Security Policy, Oct. 1991, Authors: Meyer and Garansky.
- Custodial mothers receive a support award: 79.6 percent
- Custodial fathers receive a support award: 29.9 percent
- Non-custodial mothers totally default on support: 46.9 percent
- Non-custodial fathers totally default on support: 26.9 percent

False accusations of abuse:

- 160,000 reports of suspected child abuse were reported in 1963. That number exploded to 1.7 million in 1985.
- There were more than three million reports of alleged child abuse and neglect in 1995.
- However, two million of those complaints were without foundation or false! (Source: National Center on Child Abuse and Neglect (NCCAN) Child Maltreatment 1995: Reports From the States to the National Child Abuse and Neglect Data System).

Fathers, listen up!

Don't allow your name to be listed among the deadbeat dads! Your child deserves better.

A father who does not provide for a family that he was part of creating does not have morals or a responsible enough nature to realize how difficult he is making life for his family.

Primarily used in the United States and Canada, the gender-specific deadbeat dad and deadbeat mom are commonly used by the child support agency to refer to men and women who have fathered or mothered a child and willingly fail to pay child support ordered by a family law court or statutory agency such as the Child Support Agency.

The "deadbeat dad" craze is blamed for several social ills, from poverty to welfare costs to social pathology. When the data is viewed that 6.2 million single mothers do not receive child support, we cringe in disbelief, and wonder how those dads could be so heartless to their children. How can those fathers just walk away from their responsibilities? Fathers, don't allow yourselves to be numbered among them. Consider the following:

Child Support Numbers

According to the US Census Bureau, 47.3 percent of custodial mothers (as "obligees") received all child support that they were owed and 77.5 percent received some. Additionally, 46.2 percent of custodial fathers (as "obligees") received all child support that they were owed and 74.5 percent received some.

Child support assessments are made based on a variety of formulae, and vary from state to state in the United States. According to one study 38 percent of Illinois "obligor" parents not paying child-support said they lacked the money to pay. Twenty-three percent used non-payment to protest a lack of visitation rights. Sixty-nine percent complained of no accountability over the spending of their child support money, while 13 percent said they did not want their child or children and 12 percent denied parentage.

According to a California study, 76 percent of the $14.4 billion in child support arrears in California has been attributed to "obligors" who lack the ability to pay (see Figure 1, p.5-4). In California, the "deadbeat" parents had a median annual income of $6349, arrears of $9447, ongoing support of $300 per month. One reason given for this was that 71 percent of the orders were set by default. Alternative terms for deadbeat parents who lack the ability to pay are "dead broke" and "turnip" (as in, "You can't get blood out of a turnip")

Some things every father needs to know!

- Legislation in the U.S: Main article: Bradley Amendment.
- The United States law commonly known as the Bradley Amendment was passed in 1986. It was passed with the intent to automatically trigger non-expiring liens whenever child support becomes past due. It was designed to assist children of non-supportive parents in the effort to obtain child support.
- The law overrides any state's stature of limitations. No matter how much time has passed, the state can pursue the offending parent.
- The law also disallows any judicial discretion from preventing execution, even bankruptcy judges.
- The law requires that the payment amounts be maintained without regard for the physical capability of the person owing child support (the obligor) to make the notification or regard for their awareness of the need to make the notification. Thus the obligor or payer is obligated to pay, no matter their physical capabilities or status. It is obvious the government is serious about these offenders.
- Many U.S. states have passed laws that allowed the Department of Motor Vehicles in the state to use its information to find the non-compliant parent and call them to account for their actions.
- Make note that there are now many collections-oriented sites on the Internet that mention or highlight deadbeat parents, some even showing mug shots and marking the photos as "found" in the style of the FBI's "most wanted" list.
- Further action of the US government concerning these defaulting parents: Many go to jail; others have their driving privileges suspended and contractors have business licenses revoked. Example: In the year, 2000, the state of Tennessee revoked the driver's licenses of 1,372 people who collectively owed more than $13

million USD in child support.[6] In Texas non-custodial parents behind more than three months in child-support payments can have court-ordered payments deducted from their wages, can have federal income tax refund checks, lottery winnings, or other money that may be due from state or federal sources intercepted by child support enforcement agencies. They can have licenses (including hunting and fishing licenses) suspended, and a judge may sentence a nonpaying parent to jail and enter a judgment for past due child support.

- If a parent rejects the laws, they can appeal or sue the government. Yet let it be known, on September 4, 1998, the Supreme Court of Alaska upheld a law allowing state agencies to revoke driver's licenses of parents seriously delinquent in child support obligations. And in the case of United States of America v. Sage, U.S. Court of Appeals (2nd Cir., 1996), the court upheld the constitutionality of a law allowing federal fines and up to two years imprisonment for a person willfully failing to pay more than $5,000 in child support over a year or more when said child resides in a different state from that of the non-custodial parent." Every delinquent parent of child support needs to know that legally, "they have not a leg to stand upon." So the message is, love your children and support them on your own. Don't wait until the authorities force your hands to do what you should want to do.

Main article: Bradley Amendment

- The U.S. law commonly known, as the Bradley Amendment was passed in 1986 to automatically trigger a non-expiring lien whenever child support becomes past due.
- The law overrides any state's statute of limitations.

- The law disallows any judicial discretion, even from bankruptcy judges.
- The law requires that the payment amounts be maintained without regard for the physical capability of the person owing child support (the obligor) to make the notification or regard for their awareness of the need to make the notification.
- Many U.S. states have passed laws that allowed the Department of Motor Vehicles in the state to use its information to find the non-compliant parent and call them to account for their actions.
- There are now many collections-oriented sites on the Internet that mention or highlight deadbeat parents, some even showing mug shots and marking the photos as "found" in the style of the FBI's "most wanted" list.

Action taken against defaulting parents:

In the United States, persons in arrears for child support payments are potentially subject to incarceration. Other penalties for child-support non-payment also exist. Many U.S. states suspend an individual's licenses (i.e. driver's license, business license, contractor license) or revoke passports if that individual has significant arrearage in support payments or does not consistently pay support. This authority does not extend to professionals who receive licensure through non-governmental agencies.

In the year, 2000, the state of Tennessee revoked the driver's licenses of 1,372 people who collectively owed more than $13 million USD in child support.[6] In Texas non-custodial parents behind more than three months in child-support payments can have court-ordered payments deducted from their wages, can have federal income tax refund checks, lottery winnings, or other money that may be due from state or federal sources intercepted by child support enforcement agencies. They can have licenses (including hunting and fishing licenses) suspended, and a judge may sentence a nonpaying parent to jail and enter a judgment for past due child support.

However, on September 4, 1998, the Supreme Court of Alaska upheld a law allowing state agencies to revoke driver's licenses of parents seriously delinquent in child support obligations. And in the case of United States of America v. Sage, U.S. Court of Appeals (2nd Cir., 1996), the court upheld the constitutionality of a law allowing federal fines and up to two years imprisonment for a person willfully failing to pay more than $5,000 in child support over a year or more when said child resides in a different state from that of the non-custodial parent."

Finally fathers, listen to what mothers are feeling, saying and doing about this unfortunate plight!

"He hung you and the kids out to dry. That leech sits around and spends his money on ridiculous, selfish things while the money he owes you continues accruing. You want to give your kids the world, and as his flits in and out of their lives, raising and then crushing their hopes each time (if he even bothers to show up in the first place), you see the pain welling up in their sweet, innocent eyes."

Unfortunately, this woman is not alone. Many women experience similar situation with the fathers (who do not even deserve the title) of their children. There are Internet addresses where mothers are being solicited to sign up list what they call dirt-bags and spineless parasites that will not help raise the children whose are half theirs.

Chapter X
What You Don't Know Can Hurt You!

Daddies and the devil! The biblical realities of the devil! "My people are destroyed for a lack of knowledge" (Hosea 4: 6 KJV). "And ye shall know the truth and the truth shall make ye free" (John 8: 32 KJV).

In conclusion, "What you don't know about the Devil can hurt you." In order for fathers to know their roles and be at their best, they must acknowledge the reality of the Devil and his demonic forces. Fathers and people in general who refuse to accept such realities are extremely vulnerable to the deadly assaults of the Devil. Fathers must remember back in the Garden of Eden, the man was alone for an unknown amount of time. Yet, the Devil did not attack him directly, but waited for the right opportunity through Eve, his wife.

The attack occurred later, after the creation of woman, who in Scripture has been declared the weaker vessel. "Likewise, ye husbands, dwell with them according to knowledge, giving honour unto the wife, as unto the weaker vessel, and as being heirs together of the grace of life; that your prayers be not hindered" (I Peter 3: 7).

The reference is made only to remind man of his position as a protector. As stated several times during the writing of the book, man failed to both protect and advise the woman properly. It is clear that he was present when the Devil arrived and although the devil entered into conversation with Eve, the woman, he should have intervened. For reasons unknown, he did not and the result was devastatingly disastrous. Men and fathers, make note that things have not changed much.

Today, the results are disastrous also when man does not stand or speak up and use his authority at the right time. He must know that when he gives up his God given authoritative position as protector and provider, immediately, the devil steps in. The Devil's reality must be noted and accounted for at all time and under all situations.

Further, it must be submitted that not only fathers must be made aware of the devil and his demons, but all persons on earth who possess hope of success, productivity and any measurable amount of materialistic or spiritual advancement. Those unaware or unacceptable of the Devil's existence and reality will end in devastation and tragedy. The Devil is real and deadly.

Therefore, it is imperative, crucial and of absolute necessity to both examine and absorb the reality of the devil's existence and mode of operation. All humanity needs awareness of the information that the Bible emphatically reveals about the origin, personality and intent of this being.

Listen carefully and individually, but learn collectively, God has given mankind repeated warnings about ignorance and not grasping certain crucial truth. God said to Hosea, "My people are destroyed for a lack of knowledge" (Hosea 4: 6 KJV). Second, notice too that in his day, God, the Son (Jesus) said similar words to mankind. He said, "And ye shall know the truth and the truth shall make ye free" (John 8: 32 KJV).

Ignorance in general is condemned by God, but ignorance of the devil is more condemned. In fact, it is specifically stated to be devastating to mankind's health and wellbeing. In II Cor. 2: 11 (KJV), Paul said, "Lest Satan should take advantage of us: for we are not ignorant of his devices." For your sake, for your family's sake and friends, please pay close attention to this and the next chapter warning you of the devil's intent. Your life, your family and children's lives, other loved one's lives; even your friend's lives depends upon it.

Knowledge is the first step to overcoming issues and solving problems. All of the social and psychological experts declare it so. Such as the author of American Educator's "Inflexible Knowledge: The First Step to Expertise" supports this fact.

The same is true for man in his dealings with the Devil: Knowledge is the key. Let's explore man's knowledge of the Devil and what it consist of. "The King James Version's translates the word, "Devil" from the Greek language as dia'bolos; meaning slanderer; one of the principle titles of Satan.

Another translation for Satan is Adversary, the archenemy of God and man. Adversary is the most frequently used name for the devil in the New Testament and appears over fifty times. Devil or slanderer is used over thirty times. Satan, the devil; Adversary is opposed to all that is good. His character is vile and evil and portrayed as the great deceiver."

A. The origin of Satan and Where did he come from?

In response to the question of the origin of the devil, be reminded first that Colossians 1: 16 says, "For by him (God) were all things created, that are in heaven and are in the earth, visible and invisible, whether they be thrones, or dominions, or principalities or powers: all things were created by Him and for Him."

Second, Proverb 16: 4, Solomon said, 'The Lord has made all things for Himself: Yea, even the wicked for the day of evil." In the book of Isaiah, God said, "I make peace and create evil: I the Lord do these things" (Isaiah 45: 7 KJV).

From the above passages, there's one thing that is crystal clear, "all things were created by God." When I say all things; that is exactly what I mean, all things. Note: The God who created all things is love and holy and desires such personalities surrounding him to be like him. (God will be discussed later, in more detail).

Yet in brief summary of the answer to the question, where did the devil come from? The Colossian passage informs that God created all things, including evil and wickedness, which mean, he also created the devil. Although as has been stated, when God created the devil, he was not the devil as we know him today.

Once again for clarity, he was Lucifer, the archangel of God. This was before iniquity was found in his heart. Notice real carefully the following passages for the closest explanation found from biblical exegetical research on the devil's origin are recorded within the pages of Isaiah, 14: 12-20 and Ezekiel 28: 12-19.

The proposition of Isaiah!

"How you are fallen from heaven, O Lucifer, son of the morning! How you are cut down to the ground: You who weakened the nations! For you have said in your heart: I will ascend up to heaven, I will exalt my throne above the stars of God; I will also sit on the mount of the congregation, on the farthest sides of the north: I will ascend above the heights of the clouds; I will be like the most high" (Isaiah 14: 12-14 NKJV).

The results of Lucifer's (devil) sin!

"Yet you shall be brought down to Sheol (hell), to the lowest depths of the pit. Those who see you will gaze at you, and consider you, saying: Is this the man that made the earth tremble, who shook kingdoms, Who made the world as a wilderness and destroyed its cities, who did not open the house of his prisoners?

And all the kings of the nation, all of them sleep in glory, everyone in his own house. But you are cast out of your grave, like an abominable branch, Like the garment of those who are slain, Thrust through with a sword, who goes down to the stones of the pit, like a corpse trodden under foot.

You will not be joined with them in burial, because you destroyed your land and slain your people. The brood of evil doers shall never be named" (Isaiah 14: 15-20 NKJV).

Before the exegetical process continues, note that scholars assert the words of both Ezekiel 28 and Isaiah 14 to be about Lucifer, the original name given to the Angel that would become the Devil. Ezekiel says, "Son of man, take up lamentation for the King of Tyre and say unto him, thus, saith the Lord God: You were the seal of perfection, full of wisdom and perfect in beauty. You were in Eden, the garden of God; every precious stone was your covering: The sardius, topaz, and diamond, beryl, onyx and jasper, Sapphire, turquoise and emerald with gold. The workmanship of your timbrels and pipes was prepared for you on the day you were created.

You were the anointed cherub who covers; I established you: You were on the holy mountain of God; You walked back and forth in the midst of fiery stones. You were perfect in your ways from the day you were created, 'til iniquity was found in you. By the abundance of your trading, you became filled with violence within, and you sinned.

Therefore I cast you out as a profane thing, Out of the mountain of God; And I destroyed you, O covering cherub, from the midst of the fiery stones. Your heart was lifted up because of your beauty; You corrupted your way because of your splendor; I cast you to the ground. I laid you before kings that they might gaze at you. You defiled your sanctuaries, by the multitude of your iniquities, By the iniquity of your trading; Therefore I brought fire from your midst; it devoured you. And I turned you to ashes upon the earth in the sight of all who saw you. All who knew you among the people are astonished at you: You have become a horror, And shall be no more forever" (Ezekiel 28: 12-19 NKJV).

"It must be understood that the writings from both Isaiah and Ezekiel could not refer to any mere mortal human being. Apparently God first peopled the universe or at least certain portions of it with a hierarchy of holy angels, of whom one of the highest orders was (or at least contained) the cherubim. One of them, perhaps the highest of all was "the anointed cherub that covereth," who was created beautiful and perfect in his ways.

This cherub knew that he was beautiful (which required only intelligence), but pride entered his heart and the first sin in the whole history of eternity occurred. Pride led to self-will (Isa. 14: 13-14 KJV) and self-will to rebellion. This great cherub was named Lucifer and because of his beauty, rebelled against God. He was cast down from God's throne and became the Adversary (Satan) of God and led other angels into rebellion with him.

Jude 6 says, "And the angels who did not keep their proper domain, but left their own abode, He has now reserved in everlasting chains under darkness for the judgment of the great day." II Peter 2: 4, says, "If God did not spare the angels who sinned, but cast them down to Hell and delivered them into chains of darkness, to be reserved for judgment: The Lord knoweth how deliver the godly out of temptation" (II Peter 2: 4, 9 NKJV).

Note real carefully the sequence of evil and man's sin. In the book of Genesis, the Bible declares, "In the beginning, God created the heaven and the earth. And the earth was without form and void; and darkness was upon the face of the deep." He called forth the light and made the firmament, grass, herbs, and fish of the sea, fowls of the air and cattle of the earth. God saw that it was good.

Everything God made was good. After the completion of the lower creatures, on the sixth day of creation, God created man. He made man in his image and likeness. Let them have dominion over the fish in the sea, the fowl of the air, and over the cattle, over all of the earth and the creeping thing that creeps upon the earth" (Genesis 1: 1-26 NKJV). There was nothing before God created it.

Also notice, before the man sinned; evil was already in existence. Remember God said to man, "eat of every tree, but the tree of the knowledge of good and evil; do not touch it." Therefore, evil was in existence before the "Fall," not brought on by it.

Moreover, man was created and created innocent, but with the possibility of becoming holy: the condition being, obedience. But because Satan hated God already, he hated man whom God loved and tried to destroy him. Thus as Genesis three records, the devil used craftiness and cunning to accomplish the task of mankind's destruction.

B. What the Bible says about the devil's craftiness and cunning.

Genesis, the first book of the Bible, first introduced the Devil and revealed his deceitful activity. It states, "The serpent (devil, Satan, according to Revelation 20: 2 KJV) was more subtil (crafty and cunning) than any beast of the field that the Lord God had made" (Gen. 3: 1; KJV).

The Scripture of Revelation 20: 2 was inserted to clarify the thought by many that the Serpent and the Devil are not the same (the Bible declares that they are). The conversation between the serpent and the woman, Eve, revealed the Devil's subtlety.

In fact, the Bible repeatedly issued warning after warning about the Devil's cunning and craftiness. But no one seemed to be listening. II Cor. 2: 11 (KJV), Paul said, "Lest Satan should take advantage of us: for we are not ignorant of his devices."

Ephesians 6: 11(KJV), Paul said, "To put on the whole armor of God that you may be able to stand against the wiles (strategies or cunning) of the devil." In II Corinthians 11: 3 (KJV), Paul said, "But I am afraid that as the serpent deceived Eve by its cunning, your thoughts will be led astray from a sincere and pure devotion to Christ."

Closely read the Genesis passage (Genesis 3: 1) where the Bible introduced the serpent (Devil) to man. Note: He deceived the woman (who ate and gave to the man) intending to destroy them both. They both, the woman and the man, were conned into participating in the most catastrophic event of history: "eating of the forbidden fruit" and thus disobeying God.

In great detail, the book of Genesis outlines the facts and figures of the event of the Fall. The book specifically notes that the Serpent told Eve that she would not die and that she would be as a god, if she ate from the forbidden fruit. The consequences of the con job by the devil, though, thousands of years have passed, still haunts men and women today.

The devil's action of deception brought death; disease, pain, suffering, sorrow and much more of the same into the arena of mankind existence and with every day that pass thousands of human beings meet the fate of death. We hold this truth to be self-evident that Satan is a murderer and a cold-blooded killer.

But not only a murderer, he is a mass murderer. For centuries, he has killed millions of people and so far walked away Scott-free (See Revelation 20).

Although sad, but nevertheless true and the report of Jesus confirmed it. Jesus words, as recorded by John, "Ye are of your father the devil and the lusts of your father ye will do. He was a murderer from the beginning and abode not in the truth because there is no truth in him" (John 8: 44 KJV).

Think about it, a murderer that eludes investigation and kills humans every day. He stalks the world's communities. Man's ignorance and naivety are key weapons in the Devil's arsenal for attacking and murdering mankind. While mankind looks for danger in one direction, Satan sends it from another. He just doesn't kill; he mutilates, maims and mocks.

Satan is the most dangerous serial killer the world has ever known. Even that does not fully describe his devastation and a fact that's even more sad, he's still on the loose, lurking and "seeking whom he may devour" (I Peter 5: 8 KJV).

He shows no mercy because he has none. Even his non-discrimination is a negative. He is an equal opportunist: killing men, women, boys and girls: Killing Black, White, Yellow and Brown: Killing the young and the old. He relies on man's ignorance and un-suspicion as his personal assistants in his genocidal quest.

If Satan was a human being, his face would be on police sketches posted in the banks and post offices. Our doors would be locked and the children never be let out of our sight. There would marches made on the police stations with demands that the authorities patrol the streets twenty four seven.

There would be hot lines set up for tips on the whereabouts of the mad man running wild through our cities. If Satan were a human with a reputation such as his; he would most certainly be on the FBI's most wanted list. America's Most Wanted would feature him weekly. A murderer of such devastation would never be ignored, forgotten or excused.

In fact, Satan should not receive any preferential treatment today. It should be remembered that every time a parent, child or sibling is taken to the graveyard, Satan's deception in the Garden of Eden is the cause. I don't know what that memory does to you, but it brings tears to my eyes.

The thought of the lost of everlasting life: an eternal life without pain, suffering and sorrow: The thought of the lost of a loving mother and a providing father that didn't even have to be: The thought of the loss of children that many parents, suffered through. It was sad for Adam and Eve, but, sickening for you and me.

Yet, it needs reemphasizing that at any time, God could have destroyed Satan. But for His own purpose, He did not. Paul said in Romans 16, "And the God of peace shall bruise Satan under your feet shortly" (Romans 16: 20 KJV). More specifically, the book of Revelation, chapters, 19-20, detailed God's eventual binding of the devil. First, after the battle of Armageddon, he will be bound for a thousand years in the Millennium (Revelation 20: 3).

After which, he will be loosed for a season and finally, after the battle of Gog and Magog; he will be cast into the Lake of fire for eternity (Revelation 20: 7-8). But until then, God for his own Purpose and Will, allows Satan to run loose in the world. Once again, the book of Proverbs gives evidence of this fact. Wise old Solomon said, "The Lord created all things for himself, yea, even the wicked for the day of evil" (Proverbs 16: 4 KJV).

Further, the prophet Isaiah verified, even clarified God's position. God said, "I am the Lord and there is none else, there is no God beside me: I girded thee, though thou hast not known me: That they may know from the rising of the sun, and from the west, that there is none beside me. I am the Lord and there is none else. I form the light and create darkness: I make peace and create evil: I, the Lord do all these things" (Isaiah 45: 5-7 KJV).

Both in the past and present, God used the Devil to test man's love and loyalty with evil (Job 1-2). God's hope for man remains undaunted that man would prove worthy of His love, trust and provision. The question has been asked a thousand times by believers, why did God create evil? Or better yet, why does He allow evil and the Devil to continue its reign of destruction?

Biblical exegesis reveals only one answer: God wanted man to have a choice and use the choice for God, without reservation, hesitation or intimidation. As human beings created in his image and likeness (Genesis 1:26), we value love greater when it is given freely to us.

The Beatles had a song entitled, "Money can't buy me love." "Money can buy diamond rings; money can buy all sorts of things. But I don't care too much for money because money can't buy me love." God accepts no less than love given freely from man.

In the Garden of Eden, Adam and Eve failed to choose God and allowed the Serpent (Devil) to influence them into disobedience. But in the wilderness of Jordan, Jesus succeeded and fulfilled the hope that God had for man.

Today, God is still looking for men and women to fulfill His will by obeying His voice. Matthew 4: 1 unveils the scene of Jesus' (the Second Adam's) victory: "Then was Jesus led up of the Spirit into the wilderness to be tempted of the Devil."

Please note that the Spirit of the Lord led Jesus into the wilderness to be tempted of the Devil. God led Him to the temptation with the intent for him to take advantage of the opportunity to overcome and bless the name of God. Yes, it is true that sometimes God leads man to the temptation. Yet, when He does, God leads him there for him (man) to succeed.

On the other hand, when the devil leads man to the temptation, he leads him there to fail and fall. The success or failure depends upon man's source of information. If he listens to public opinion and his own knowledge, he fails. But if he listens to the Word of God, he succeeds.

Please, note the difference. Solomon reminds man to, "Trust in the LORD with all your heart and lean not on your own understanding; in all your ways acknowledge him, and he will make your paths straight. Do not be wise in your own eyes; fear the LORD and shun evil" (Proverb 3: 5-7 NIV).

Matthew's Gospel says, "And when he had fasted forty days and forty nights, afterwards he was hungry" (Matt. 4: 2 KJV). The devil knows much about man's condition. The text points out that he knew the point of Jesus' weakest state. The devil and the demons are aware of you and me. It is imperative that we acknowledge his determination and perseverance to cause us pain and suffering.

The scripture says, "When the tempter came to him, he said, if you are the Son of God, command that these stones be made bread" (Matt. 4: 3 KJV).

Once again, Satan tried to cast doubt into the mind of Jesus in hope of getting Him to try and prove his identity. A tactic used by him on mankind for the last six thousand years. In fact, it was the first and the same tactic he used on Adam and Eve back in the Garden of Eden (Genesis 3: 1-5 NKJV).

The Serpent told Eve, God knows who you are and what you are capable of becoming, a god, that's why he doesn't want you to eat from the Tree of the knowledge of good and evil. Eve was an easy sell on the idea of eating and becoming a god because she wanted God-like power. She wanted to do things her way. She really did not want God and anybody else to stand in the way of her desires.

Basically Eve wanted Self-Determination where she could determine her own consequences instead of another. However, this is one of the attributes of the Almighty God. Yet, mankind still has the same conflict, even as this book is being read: There is a conflict between self-rule and God-rule.

Everyday man faces the conflict of having to choose, do I tithe to God or do I keep the money for myself? Do I get dressed and drive myself to the church or do I rest and relax? Do I do this for me or do I do that for God and others? The examples are long and in-exhaustive. But in short, the question of consequence is; do I give in to the lusts of the flesh, or to the "words that proceed out of the mouth of God" (Matt. 4: 4 KJV)?

Also, "Jesus replied: "'Love the Lord your God with all your heart and with all your soul and with all your mind.' This is the first and greatest commandment. And the second is like it: 'Love your neighbor as yourself.' All the Law and the Prophets hang on these two commandments" (Matt. 22: 37-40 NIV).

Obviously, the Devil wants you to give in to the desires of the flesh. The Devil knows that when you give in to the desires of the flesh and withhold your tithes and offerings, God will withhold your blessings. Recorded in the book of Malachi, God said to Israel, "Bring the whole tithe into the storehouse, that there may be food in my house.

Test me in this," says the LORD Almighty, "and see if I will not throw open the floodgates of heaven and pour out so much blessing that you will not have room enough for it. I will prevent pests from devouring your crops, and the vines in your fields will not cast their fruit," says the LORD Almighty" (Malachi 3: 10-11 NIV).

The Devil knows that when you stay away from the church worship, you not only miss worship of the Lord, but the fellowship of fellow believers that's necessary for spiritual growth. Paul said. "Let us not give up meeting together, as some are in the habit of doing, but let us encourage one another-and all the more as you see the Day approaching" (Hebrews 10: 25 NIV).

When wrestling with the flesh and the prince of this world (Satan), my recommendation is to consider the methodology of Jesus and withstand the Devil's influence by relying on the Word of God. "But he answered and said, it is written, man shall not live by bread alone, but by every word that proceeds out of the mouth of God" (Matt. 4: 4 KJV). Mankind is to live by God's commands and instructions if he is to find happiness and fulfillment.

Jesus said, "He that hath my commandments and keepeth them, he it is that loveth me: and he that loveth me shall be loved of my Father, and I will love him and manifest myself unto him" (John 14: 21 KJV). Man needs to be reminded that obedience to the devil in any form or fashion is disobedience to God and will lead to certain destruction (John 10: 10 KJV).

"Then the devil took him up into the holy city, set him on the pinnacle of the temple" (the tradition being, the temple at Jerusalem was 180 feet high to its peak.") 16 And said, to him, "If you are the Son of God, throw yourself down, for it is written: he shall give his angels charge over you and in their hands they shall bear you up, lest you dash your foot against a stone" (Matthew 4: 5-6 NKJV).

Again, the lying and deceitful nature of the devil is revealed. Make note that Devil also knows God's word. The verse, the devil quoted was from the ninety-first Psalm. Yet the devil intentionally misquoted it. The Psalmist said, "He shall give his angels charge over you to keep you in all thy ways" (Psalm 91: 11-12 NKJV). Satan conveniently left out the words, "To keep you in all thy ways," or the ways of God and the angel will bear thee up: A deliberate strategy to misquote the words of God and mislead Jesus. The commands of Jesus and the advice of the leadership of Christianity are for the people of the world and specifically for the Body of Christ to study the Word of God for themselves. Paul says, "Study to show thyself approved unto God, a workman that needeth not to be ashamed, rightly dividing the word of truth. But shun profane and vain babblings: for they will increase unto more ungodliness" (II Tim. 2: 15-16 KJV).

If there is any hope to defeat the Devil, it has and will always be through the Word of God. For if the Devil has the audacity to attempt to mislead Jesus with the Scripture, man must know that he will tempt us as well. "Jesus said unto him again, "It is written, you shall not tempt the Lord your God" (Matt. 4: 7 KJV).

"Again, the Devil took him up into an exceedingly high mountain and showed him all of the kingdoms of the world and their glory. And he said to Him, "All these things will I give unto you, if you will fall down and worship me" (Matthew 4: 9 NKJV).

Luke's rendering states that Satan offered Jesus all of the power and glory of the kingdom that has been delivered to him" (Luke 4: 6 NKJV). The key difference between Luke and Matthew's version is that Luke indicates the power and glory of the world was given to Satan from somebody; obviously, God.

Allow me the privilege to affirm and confirm the fact that Satan has no power or ownership apart from God; an important reality of theology. The Psalmist declared, "The earth is the Lords and the fullness thereof; the world and they that dwell therein. For he founded it upon the seas and established it upon the floods" (Psalm 24: 1-2 KJV).

The book of Job also confirms this fact. Satan went to God for permission to attack Job on every occasion. God gave permission, but with direct directions how far the Devil was to go in the attack on Job. In other words, God holds the reigns of the world in the palm of his hands. Rejoice humans, again I say rejoice. God is in charge, not the Devil.

"Then Jesus said to him, away with you Satan! For it is written, "You shall worship the Lord your God and him only you shall serve. Then the devil left him and behold angels came and ministered to him" (Matthew 4: 10-11 Nor). However, Luke 4: 13 informs us that the "Devil left Jesus only for a season:" Another indication (along with the Job, Peter and other's situation) that the devil is consistently coming into and going out of man's domain.

Before leaving the temptation of Jesus out in the wilderness of Jordan, there are several key observations that are worth their weight in gold. The temptation followed the same pattern that the Serpent used back in the Garden of Eden. Rick Warren says that Satan always follow the same pattern of temptation. He identified it and labeled it into a four step pattern. It just so happened that all of the components begin with the letter D.

First, he says Satan identifies a "Desire" within the person: A weakness and vulnerability of some kind that he can work with. Satan then creates "Doubt" in God or in God's word. This doubt within the human family destroys their confidence and leaves the doors of insecurity and disbelief open.

Once the door of doubt and disbelief are opened, Satan accesses the rooms of Deception. Remember Satan is an expert in the field of cunning and deception. The Bible repeatedly reminds us of Satan's "subtlety" (Gen. 3: 1 & Eph. 6: 11).

Finally, according to Rick Warren; the deception of the Devil leads to the fourth D; Disobedience.33 Make note that disobedience is the big concern of God. The citing of Mr. Warren's Pattern is to further affirm the main thesis of the book that Satan is behind temptation.

Even more to the point, James said, "Let no man say when he is tempted, I am tempted of God: for God cannot be tempted with evil, neither tempteth he any man: But every man is tempted, when he is drawn away of his own lust, and enticed. Then when lust hath conceived, it bringeth forth sin: and sin, when it is finished, bringeth forth death" (James 1: 13-15 KJV).

To summarize what has been said up to now on the question, "Did the Devil make me do it?" Briefly, let us review the over whelming Scriptural passages related to the subject. The Bible says, "Then, he called his 12 disciples unto him, and gave them power and authority over all devils, and to cure diseases" (Luke 9: 1 KJV). Mankind has the power over all Devils.

"And the seventy returned again with joy, saying, Lord, even the devils are subject unto us through thy name. And he said unto them, I beheld Satan as lightening fall from heaven. Behold, I give you power to tread upon serpents and scorpions and over all the power of the enemy: (Luke 10: 17-19a KJV). Mankind has power over the enemy.

Jesus said, "Simon, Simon, Satan hath desireth to have you that he may sift you as wheat, but I have prayed for thee" (Luke 22: 31 KJV). Jesus prayed for mankind to overcome the Devil and God grant's Jesus' prayers.

Satan said, "But put forth thine hand now, and touch all that he hath, and he will curse thee to thy face. And the LORD said unto Satan, Behold, all that he hath is in thy power; only upon himself put not forth thine hand" (Job 1: 11-12 KJV). God has Satan under subjection on man's behalf.

Paul said, "There hath no temptation taken you, such as is common to man: but God is faithful who will not suffer you to be tempted above that ye are able; but with every temptation also make a way to escape, that ye may be able to bear it. Wherefore, my dearly beloved, flee from idolatry" (I Corinth. 10: 13-14 KJV).

With every temptation, there is a way for man to escape. There you have it, the biblical report is in. Satan CAN NOT do anything to the child of God without God's permission (Job 1-2).

Therefore, the answer to the question, did the devil make me do it, is absolutely not: No way and no how: A resounding "no." Let it be proclaimed from the rooftop, the Devil cannot make any person do anything. The Bible says, "Submit yourselves therefore to God. Resist the devil, and he will flee from you" (James 4: 7 KJV).

Mankind has the power to resist. Thank God, Thank God; Thank God. Therefore, make "temptation a stepping stone rather than a stumbling block. An opportunity rather than an obstacle: A testimony rather than a test: A privilege rather than a protest. Temptation is an opportunity to do right as it is to do wrong. Temptation simply provides the choice." 25 Let us make the right choice; to glorify God and shame the devil.

Now that the question, *did the devil make me do it?*, has been thoroughly explored, Biblically analyzed and answered with a resounding *no*, there are a few other questions remaining that need addressing. Such as, if the devil did not make me do it, who did? Does God make me do what I do or some other entity? Do I make myself do what I do and if I do, whose influence am I under, if any?

The jury of history has rendered its verdict on the first question with a resounding, *no*. Now the book moves to its present case on the second question: does God make me do what I do? If you want to read more on this subject, obtain a copy of Dr. Lomax's book, "Did the Devil Make Me Do It? But first, in summarizing the present chapter, here are some of the Biblical highlights that one should now be conscious of!

The Devil's intentions toward mankind:

A. Jesus said, "The thief comest but for to steal, kill and destroy." (John 10:10 KJV). The devil is the thief and his intentions are clear. He wants man broke and busted, dead and lost.
B. Peter said, "Be sober, be vigilant: because your adversary, the Devil, walketh about like a roaring lion, seeking whom he may devour: whom resist steadfast in the faith, knowing that the same afflictions are accomplished in your brethren that are in the world" (I Peter 5: 8-9 KJV).

Peter's instructions to man is to be sober and vigilant. Man can defeat the devil, but needs to be at his best. "He is at his best when he is watchful, alert and exercises self-control." 17

The reason for this caution, mankind needs to be aware that there is an adversary, called the devil, lurking. Remember the words of Peter, "He walketh about, like a roaring lion, seeking whom he may devour." In other words, this enemy, like a wild animal is roaming the streets and looking for any person to kill and eat. So man better be aware.

In II Timothy, Paul advised Timothy that "there were some that needed to recover themselves out of the snare of the devil who were taken captive by him at his will"(II Tim 2: 26). The devil is not only walking about in the world seeking, but is also setting traps for men and women. Even today, some men and women have fallen victim to the traps set by Satan. Paul warned man about a behind the scene, manipulating devil.

The devil's will is clear. It is to take captive (or control of) as many human beings as he desires. Even though Paul warned about it, he also gave hope that man can recover and escape from the captivity of the devil. In other words, when the Devil knocks you down, you don't have to stay down. Recover, break-loose and escape. Remember "failure is not being knocked down, it's staying down" (Source Unknown).

The book of Zechariah informed mankind that "the guiding angel showed Joshua the high priest standing before the angel of the Lord and Satan standing at his right hand ready to oppose him. And the Lord said to Satan, the Lord rebukes you Satan! The Lord who has chosen Jerusalem rebukes you! Is this not a brand plucked from the fire" (Zech. 3: 1-2 NKJV)?

Exegesis reports that Joshua the high priest was preparing to go to battle. The angel of the Lord was there to assist him in the victory. Yet the prophet Zechariah made note that Satan was also there standing with them to resist and oppose their efforts.

Once again, Satan appeared before the angelic host to instigate havoc upon the human family. There should not be any doubt concerning his purpose of destruction. But, thank God for his intervention. He intervened and rebuked Satan. He said, I have decided to have mercy on the city of Jerusalem, Joshua and the nation. Though it was like pulling burning sticks from the fire.

The devil's influence and control over mankind: Both in the Old Testament and the New Testament, the devil demonstrated influence and control over man.

No one can forget the serpent's (devil) influence over Adam and Eve in the Garden of Eden (Genesis 3: 1KJV). It has been repeatedly discussed and will not be here, but must be listed. It was by far the most catastrophic event in the history of man and the one with the most long lasting ramifications.

"Satan stood up against Israel to provoke David to number Israel" (I Chron. 21: 1-3 KJV). Even though Joab protested for God, David did as Satan inspired. The Devil has a history of provoking and inspiring humans to go against the will of God. Men and women need to be mindful of the agenda of the devil. Satan doesn't do anything for the advancement of mankind. You can take that fact to the bank and deposit it.

The book of Job's account verifies Satan's (devil) mission. God asked him, whence cometh thou Satan? He answered, from going to and fro and up and down in the earth. Eventually, he asked God for permission to bring destruction on Job and his family (Job, chapters 1-2 KJV).

The New Testament records John's words, "And supper being ended, the devil having already put into the heart of Judas Iscariot, Simon's son to betray him" (John 13:2 NKJV). Further, in the text, John says, "Now, after the piece of bread, Satan entered him. Then Jesus said to him, what you do, do quickly" (John 13: 27 NKJV).

He then having received the sop went immediately out: and it was night (John 13: 30 KJV). The point being that after Satan entered him; he went out and betrayed Jesus to the multitudes.

Physician Luke records Jesus saying, "So ought not this woman, being a daughter of Abraham, whom Satan hath bound- think of it for eighteen years, be loosed on the Sabbath" (Luke 13: 16 NKJV).

Exegesis reveals the woman had an issue of blood for eighteen years. In the eyes of Jesus, sickness was the result of Satan. There are many scripture passages of sickness that Jesus concluded were the result of Satanic or demonic activity.

Mark five records one such occasion. The demoniac man was crying and cutting himself with stones. Society thought that he was crazy, howbeit; Jesus concluded that he was possessed with unclean spirits. He called them out of the man and sure enough the man was made well (Mark 5: 1-19 NKJV).

"But he turned and said to Peter, "Get thee behind me, Satan! You are an offense to me, for you are not mindful of the things of God, but the things of men" (Matt. 16: 23 NKJV).

"But Peter said, Ananias, why hast Satan fill your heart to lie to the Holy Ghost and keep back part of the price of the land for thyself"(Acts 5: 3 NKJV).

"Be angry and sin not. Do not let the sun go down on your wrath, nor give place to the Devil (Eph. 4: 26-27 KJV).

"In this the children of God and the children of the Devil are manifest: Whosoever does not practice righteousness is not of God, nor is he that does not love his brother (I John 3: 10 NKJV).

"Jesus said, haven't I chosen you 12 and one of you is a devil" (John 6: 70 KJV)?

"In your anger do not sin:" Do not let the sun go down while you are still angry, and do not give the devil a foothold. He who has been stealing must steal no longer, but must work, doing something useful with his own hands that he may have something to share with those in need.

Do not let any unwholesome talk come out of your mouths, but only what is helpful for building others up according to their needs, that it may benefit those who listen. And do not grieve the Holy Spirit of God, with whom you were sealed for the day of redemption" (Eph. 4: 27-30 NIV).

"You are a child of the devil and an enemy of everything that is right" (Acts 13: 10 KJV).

The devil's attributes: it is important to know as much as possible about the devil in order to recognize him. The importance of this recognition cannot be over emphasized. It is a life and death issue. Recognize him in time and live life to the fullest. Fail and allow him to slip up on you and death can result. Hebrews 2: 10, says, "the devil had the power of death, but Jesus came to destroy him" (Hebrews 2: 10 NIV).

Sinner: it needs noting that the devil was the first sinner. In fact, sin began in the devil and is of the devil. It needs to be recognized that sin came into existence as a result of Lucifer's (devil) rebellion. John said, "He that sins is of the devil: for the devil has sinned from the beginning. For this purpose the Son of God was manifested that he might destroy the works of the devil" (I John 3: 8 KJV).

Destroyer! Jesus said to Peter, Simon, Simon, behold Satan desires to have you that he may sift (Grind) you as wheat, but I am praying for you" (Luke 22: 31 KJV). Peter says, "Be sober: Be vigilant because your adversary the devil walketh about seeking whom he may devour" (I Peter 5: 8 KJV). Satan said, "But stretch out your hand and strike everything he has, and he will surely curse you to your face" (Job 1: 11 NIV).

Paul said, "God will give them repentance, to the acknowledgment of the truth; and they that come to their senses and escape the snare of the Devil, who are taken captive by him at his will" (I Tim. 2: 25-26 NKJV).

Thief!

"The Thief comest for to steal, kill and to destroy" (John 10: 10 KJV).

Jesus said, "And the enemy that sows them is the devil; and he comes and steals them away" (Matt. 13: 39 KJV). Satan comes and steals the word of God away from hearers that was sown (Mark 4: 15 KJV).

Satan does not want any one saved. This is a reference to the word of God being planted into the potential believer. Satan makes an attempt to snatch up the word before it sinks into the believer's heart: Once again revealing the devil's activity to interfere with the salvation of mankind.

Con Artist! "Now the serpent was more crafty than any of the wild animals the LORD God had made" (Gen. 3: 1 NIV).

But I am afraid that just as Eve was deceived by the serpent's cunning, your minds may somehow be led astray from your sincere and pure devotion to Christ" (II Cor. 11: 3 NIV). "Put on the full armor of God so that you can take your stand against the devil's schemes. For our struggle is not against flesh and blood, but against the rulers, against the authorities; against the powers of this dark world and against the spiritual forces of evil in the heavenly realms" (Eph. 6: 11-12 NIV).

Full of Pride: "Not a novice, lest being puffed up with pride, he falls into the same condemnation as the devil" (I Tim. 3: 6 KJV). In the fourth chapter of Matthew, the Devil demonstrated the characteristic of pride. He tried to get Jesus to jump off of the temple in the sight of mankind and allow the angels to sweep him up.

This event would be a grand demonstration to the world of Jesus' power and he would feel great pride and joy. However, let mankind take note and remember Jesus' response, "It is written, Thou shalt not tempt the Lord thy God" (Matt. 4: 7 KJV).

How to avoid the devil: "Submit yourselves therefore to God and resist the Devil and he will flee from you" (James 4: 7 NKJV).

"In your anger do not sin:" Do not let the sun go down while you are still angry, and do not give the devil a foothold" (Eph. 4: 27 NIV).

Devil works miracles. "For they are the spirits of devils, working miracles, which go forth unto the kings of the earth and of the whole world; to gather them to the battle of that great day of God, Almighty" (Rev 16: 14 KJV).

The final analysis of the question, "<u>Who Is The Devil</u>," has been answered. Clearly from all that has been clarified and verified, the answer is no, the devil did not make man do it. It was demonstrated in the book of Job; and time and time again ever since. The devil cannot make man do anything. Man is under the protective hand of the almighty God.

Yet, there are other questions remaining. Such as, if the devil did not make me do it, who did? Did God make me do what I did or some other entity? Did I make myself do it and if I did, whose influence was I under, if any?

The first question has been answered. Now the book moves to answer the second question. Does God make me do what I do? This is the question that will be addressed in the next chapter, entitled, who is God?

But before putting the book down, write down at least three points of information learned from the above chapter. For example, what was the name given the angel that later became the Devil? In what books of the Bible is the Devil spoken of by name? What is the Devil's purpose for humanity?

1. _____
2. _____
3. _____

What is the final analysis of it all?

Fathers, you can receive the greatest reward that life has to offer. It is in your hands. Do right by the children and they will do right by you! The author of the book has, as well as many others. On the other hand, you can be numbered among the fathers that either abandoned or deserted their families, the choice is yours! But the subject will come up again.

May God bless you for reading this book. If you apply what you read, I know He will. I gladly join the song writer that sings, "He keeps on blessing me over and over again."